Justice for Pro Se's

Justice for Pro Se's

☙❧

Richard A. Posner

© Richard A. Posner | April 3, 2018

ISBN-13: 978-1985724433

ISBN-10: 198572443X

Contents

Preface vii

Introduction 1

Let's Make My Company Nationwide 35

Three Lists 76

The Mission of My Company: A Statement 115

Of Finance and Organization 130

Coda: How Team Posner Inc. Molted into
    Justice for Pro Se's and Then into
    Posner Center of Justice for Pro Se's 137

Web Preview 138

Appendix: Judge Gilman's Writing Rules 149

Index 175

This book—the 70th book written by Richard Posner—is dedicated in gratitude to:

The members of the Posner Center of Justice for Pro Se's, formerly known as Justice for Pro Se's,

And our clients—and critics—and all who have helped, including

The invaluable George W. Rumsey, President of Computer Resource Center, Inc.

and

Amazon CreateSpace, our publisher

April 2018

Preface: Amending the Second (March 10, 2018) Edition of *Justice for Pro Se's* by Richard A. Posner

The first edition of *Justice for Pro Se's* was published by Amazon CreateSpace (the publishing arm of Amazon) on February 19 of this year. Reading it over after it was published, I found nontrivial errors of both commission and omission, and I tried to correct them in a second edition, the edition of March 10. I was cautious, however, and so rather than order a number of copies of the second edition, as I had done with the first edition, I ordered only one, which arrived on Monday, March 19, the day *before* Amazon had told me it would arrive (this is typical of Amazon, which prides itself on the rapidity of its deliveries).

  I read it, and quickly realized that it was already out of date—that like its predecessor it had nontrivial errors of both commission and omission. And so I decided to order no additional copies of the second edition, but instead to revise it to correct all the errors, and only then to publish it en masse.

* * *

So much for the preface. Let me now turn to the pages of the second edition where I find errors either of commission or omission—or of both.

The introduction, which follows directly on the preface, is generally accurate; it explains briefly my two books that preceded the two editions of *Justice for Pro Se's* preceding the present one (which is thus the fifth book, though the fourth was published in only one copy!) that I have published since I retired from the court of appeals of the Seventh Circuit on September 2nd of last year (2017) because of the court's failure, as I believed, to treat pro se litigants fairly.

There is only one error in the second edition's Introduction: on page 3, in the third line of the first full paragraph, March 1 should be March 10, the actual date of publication of the second (the one-copy) edition of *Justice for Pro Se's*.

There is, however, a major omission in the Introduction, one I just became cognizant of as a result of a conference call on (March 23) with among others Selvyn Seidel, a very wealthy New York financier who is a strong supporter of my company, but has persuaded me to make certain changes, beginning with the name of my company at the top of page 4:

The Posner Center of Justice for Pro Se's

Richard A. Posner
March 23, 2018

Introduction

On September 2, 2017, I retired as a judge of the U.S. Court of Appeals for the Seventh Circuit, which embraces Illinois, Indiana, and Wisconsin. I had served on the court for 35 and 2/3 years; I retired because my court was not treating pro se appellants fairly (pro se is a Latin term meaning "for oneself"; in law, pro se signifies a litigant who is not represented by a lawyer). Soon after my retirement I published two books expressing my concerns for the mistreatment of pro se's: *Reforming the Federal Judiciary: My Former Court Needs to Overhaul Its Staff Attorney Program and Begin Televising Its Oral Arguments* (published by CreateSpace, the superb publishing arm of Amazon, on September 7, 2017), and *Improving the Federal Judiciary: Staff Attorney Programs, the Plight of the Pro Se's, and the Televising of Oral Arguments* (2d ed.—sequel and reference work—published by CreateSpace on December 4, 2017). The "synoptic preface to the second edition," followed by a brief discussion of CreateSpace—two short pieces that kick off the second edition—constitute a helpful introduction to my project by explaining the failure of my court to do justice to pro se's. I also invite readers' attention to chapters 3 through 5 of the second book (*Improving the Federal Judiciary*)—a 77-page account of efforts by my company and a number of other companies to assist pro se's with their legal problems.

More important than either of the two books is that shortly after my retirement from the court I created and own and direct a company devoted to helping pro se's and other persons disserved by the judiciary. The name of the company, formerly Justice for Pro Se's, is now the Posner Center of Justice for Pro Se's. This new book, though shorter than its two predecessors, provides both more detailed and more up-to-date information about the company, information that I believe will prove of great value to the members of my company, to pro se's generally, to other litigants who need assistance in pressing their claims, and to lawyers and nonlawyer advisors committed to assisting pro se's and other claimants in need of unconventional help to obtain justice. Initially I ordered 100 copies of the new book from Amazon, intending to mail them to the members of my company. But shortly after ordering them I realized that there were errors in the draft. I could not correct them in the copies that were in the hands of Amazon, but as I did not and do not think that the market for the book would be limited to the 100 copies I had ordered, I decided—with the concurrence of George Rumsey, the technical expert who has provided enormous assistance to me with regard to this book as he had done with regard to the previous books in this series—to revise the book and order 200 copies of the revision. This book, new though published very shortly after the first, the 100-copies edition, is the result of that decision.

This is the fourth book in the sequence that began with *Reforming the Federal Judiciary*, published on September 7 of last year (2017). The four constitute what is called a tetralogy (from the Greek *tetralogia*), defined as a sequence of four related works, often of a dramatic or literary character. The second in the tetralogy, *Improving the Federal Judiciary*, was published on December 4, and at 433 pages is much the longest of the four books. The first two focus on the staff attorney program of the Seventh Circuit Court of Appeals (the court from which I retired on September 2 of last year)—the program that largely governs the handling of appeals by pro se's—litigants who do not have lawyers—and on my efforts to improve the program for the benefit of pro se's in face of fierce opposition by the chief judge of the court, Diane Wood, and the court's other members, all of whom sided with her against me. The two books also discussed the question whether to allow the televising of the court's oral arguments; I thought it should be allowed but as far as I know it is not yet allowed

The last two books in the tetralogy, books 3 and 4, both bearing the same name: *Justice for Pro Se's*, were published on February 19 and March 10, 2018, respectively. They differ from the first two in being considerably shorter but also and more important in focusing entirely on my new company, started shortly after my resignation from the Seventh Circuit, which as the name of the company implies assists pro se's who have valid legal claims—assists them sometimes by providing lawyers for them and sometimes by teaching them to be their own courtroom lawyers. This fifth book is only slightly longer, but considerably more comprehensive, than the third and fourth.

I should mention that my original idea for a new name of the company (previously called Team Posner Inc.) was The Justice League, a name suggested by a client of the firm, Ted Martin, but it turns out that my using the name for my company might infringe trademarks of other companies, including The Justice League, the Pro Se Justice League, and The League of Justice for Pro Se's. And so I settled on Justice for Pro Se's, and now renamed the Posner Center of Justice for Pro Se's.

The Posner Center of Justice for Pro Se's
Richard A. Posner
March 23, 2018

To complete this introduction I need to explain my company now renamed **The Posner Center of Justice for Pro Se's** (its previous name was simply **Justice for Pro Se's**) at the suggestion of Selvyn Seidel, the prominent New York financier who is the chairman of the Center's (i.e., the company's) board of directors, as explained later in the book.

On September 2nd of last year (2017) I retired from the court of appeals of the Seventh Circuit after 35 and 2/3 years, including 7 years as chief judge, because I believed, and still believe, that pro se's, which is to say litigants without lawyers, were not receiving adequate assistance—a fair shake—from the court. I had already begun writing a book explaining my concerns for pro se's, and upon retiring from the court and having therefore a lot of free time I finished the book quickly and it was published—remarkably—on September 7, 2017, only five days after my retirement, by Amazon CreateSpace, the super-efficient publishing arm of the Amazon company. In the ensuing months I published three more books; a fourth (actually a fifth—a revision of a fourth that I thought inadequate and therefore decided not to publish) will be published shortly.

From the outset I had thought that my company (now the Posner Center) would grow and eventually need a lot of money, which could be obtained only by donations. To that end I authorized a team from the University of Chicago Law School to help me obtain 501(c)(3) status for my company (now the Center), which would enable it to obtain charitable donations without tax liability either for me or my Center or for the donors.

The later books explain the company (now to be called the Center); I shall give an abbreviated description of it here. Beginning very soon after my retirement from the court, I created a

INTRODUCTION

company (the Center's predecessor) dedicated to assisting pro se's. I hired a number of people to staff it, mainly but not only lawyers—for there are many nonlawyers who are knowledgeable about law and about the problems and needs of pro se's.

At present the Center has about 80 representatives (as I sometimes term the people I've hired), consisting of lawyers and nonlawyers, distributed across 27 states. I hope eventually to have representatives in all 50 states plus the nation's offshore possessions, such as the Commonwealth of Puerto Rico, the Commonwealth of the Northern Mariana Islands, American Samoa, and the U.S. Virgin Islands.

I make clear to the people I hire that I do not expect them to work for my Center full time. Many of them are lawyers with a legal practice and/or a law-firm commitment, and those who are not lawyers usually have other jobs. All I ask of them is that they devote a few hours a month to helping one or two or maybe three pro se's obtain justice, whether by representing pro se's in court or by training them to be their own courtroom lawyers. That often is the best way of obtaining justice for a pro se; for juries more than judges tend to be impressed by a lone litigant standing up against a gaggle of lawyers representing the pro se's opponent or opponents.

From the outset I had thought that my company (now the Posner Center) would grow and eventually need a lot of money, which could be obtained only by donations. To that end I authorized a team from the University of Chicago Law School to help me obtain 501(c)(3) status for my company (now the Center), which would enable it to obtain charitable donations without tax liability either for me or my Center or for the donors

I do not at present pay my representatives (whom I frequently call volunteers because their work for the company is mainly pro bono, that is, not compensated), partly for lack of money (the Center has none as yet) and partly because I view their efforts to help pro se's as pro bono service—service for the sake of the good rather than for the sake of compensation. But this may well change as the Center expands.

Recently I have begun grouping the states in which I have or hope soon to have representatives into regions and appointing a Regional Director (at present without compensation) for each region. In a division of responsibilities with Brian Vukadinovich, an outstanding member of the Center, we shall be monitoring the activities of the Regional Directors and of the Center's representatives in the Directors' regions—again without compensation, at least for the present.

There will be a two-tier monitoring structure for resolving the problem. The lower tier will be monitoring of members' activities by Regional Directors (they and their monitoring activities are discussed at length later in the book), who will be expected to keep tabs on the company members in their districts, to maintain relations with the leading law firms and lawyers in their districts and sometimes invite the lawyers to join our company, to learn as much as they can about the pro se's in their districts, and to share information with other pro bono organizations.

The higher tier, involving review of the reports of the Regional Directors, will be administered jointly by Brian Vukadinovich and me, and will involve close contact between us and the Regional Directors and also a numbering of the regions. We shall begin by parceling out the Regions between us; our tentative decision is for Brian to handle his Region, which we'll call Region 1, embracing Indiana and the part of Illinois that lies south of Chicago, plus Chicago, which we'll call Region 2 (the Regional Director there is Sakina Carbide). Region 3 will be Jonathan Zell's region, encompassing Ohio, Michigan, Kentucky, and West Virginia. Region 4 will be Matthew Dowd's, encompassing the District of Columbia, Maryland, Virginia, North Carolina, and South Carolina. Region 5 will be Missouri; the Regional Director is Alan Popkin. Region 6 is the very large region centered on Texas; Patrick Thesing is the Regional Director. Region 7 will be New Jersey and Alaska; the Regional Director is Paul Clark. I will handle Regions 3 through 7 for the time being. I am optimistic that there will soon be a Region 8 consisting of Florida, Georgia, and Alabama, and a Region 9 consisting of Kansas, Colorado, and perhaps other western states. Brian Vukadinovich and I will divide these. The nine regions are just a beginning, as is the monitoring of them by Brian and me.

The following recent press release provides a further description of the new firm:

FOR IMMEDIATE RELEASE

March 25, 2018

Contact Person:
Richard A. Posner
President, The Posner Center of Justice for Pro Se's
Tel.: 773-955-1351
E-mail: rposner62@gmail.com

The Renamed "Posner Center of Justice for Pro Se's" Is Open for Business

CHICAGO, Illinois—Richard A. Posner has announced the renaming of his nationwide pro bono legal-services organization for assisting pro se litigants. Formerly named "Justice for Pro Se's," and before that "Team Posner," it now goes by the name "The Posner Center of Justice for Pro Se's."

On September 2, 2017, Judge Posner retired after almost 36 years as a judge of the Court of Appeals for the Seventh Circuit (including 7 years as its chief judge) because, as he says: "I believed, and still believe, that pro se's, which is to say litigants without lawyers, are not receiving a fair shake from the courts." Actually, it is even worse than that, as Judge Posner further explains: "Many judges are hostile to pro se's, seeing them as a kind of 'trash' not even worth the courts' time."

Ever the prolific writer, since his retirement Judge Posner has published four books explaining pro ses' need for legal assistance and setting out the framework for a legal-services organization that would provide that assistance free of charge. He then created what is now called the Posner Center of Justice for Pro Se's (formerly called just Justice for Pro Se's), a nationwide organization of lawyers and non-lawyers who assist deserving pro se litigants free of charge with their cases. The Center now has some 80 lawyers and non-lawyer advisors distributed across 27 states, but expects eventually to have representatives in all 50 states plus the nation's offshore possessions, such as the Commonwealth of Puerto Rico, the Commonwealth of the Northern Mariana Islands, American Samoa, and the U.S. Virgin Islands.

Although individuals have been representing themselves in court since the beginning of the Republic, it is only recently that the courts and the bar associations have begun to make accommodations for them—a trend that the Posner Center of Justice for Pro Se's is building upon. As Judge Posner points out: "The need of pro se litigants for legal assistance is obvious. Few people can afford to pay an attorney for the years that a lawsuit often takes to get resolved. Also, the U.S. legal system is so complicated and confusing that no layperson can successfully get through its maze unaided by expert legal assistance."

A unique aspect of the Center is that while its lawyers will sometimes take over the pro se's cases and represent the pro se's in court, equally or even more often it will assist the pro se's behind the scenes to enable them to successfully represent themselves—to be in effect their own courtroom lawyers. For, as Judge Posner has explained, "Representing oneself in court is often the best way for a pro se to obtain justice. Unlike judges, juries tend to be impressed by a lone litigant standing up against a gaggle of lawyers."

At present none of the Center's representatives is paid (although that may change). But not for Judge Posner, who has

INTRODUCTION   −9−

announced "This work is a labor of love and I will not accept even a single penny for my work on behalf of pro se's."

A few of the legal luminaries from academia who have joined the Center are law professors Lawrence Lessig (Harvard), Abbe Gluck (Yale), Rebecca Stone (UCLA), Daniel Klerman (USC), Shon Hopwood (Georgetown), Sandra Aistars (George Mason University), Christopher Ogolla (Savannah Law School), as well as Eric Posner, Alison Siegler, Thomas Miles, Joshua Avratin, David Zarfes, and William Landes (all from the University of Chicago).

Although Judge Posner's firm (which dates back to September 2017 though it has altered over time) has already helped many pro se's, as Judge Posner has explained, "We are just touching the surface, for there are reliably believed to be at least a million pro se's in the United States. Many of those pro se's, however, don't realize they can obtain legal assistance. Therefore, I will continue to work to get the message out that our organization exists, and then try to assist as many deserving pro se's as possible."

# # #

A company so conceived and organized needs some money but not necessarily a great deal. I suspect that so far my phone bill (which I pay for out of my own pocket) is the Center's principal expense, but an expense borne only by me. This will change, however; the Center's growth will inevitably produce an increase in the Center's expenses and hence in its need for money. And that need will have to be satisfied mainly by donations to the Center by members of the board of directors and by other well wishers.

From the outset I had thought that my company (now the Posner Center) would grow and eventually need a *lot* of money, which could be obtained only by donations. To that end I authorized a team from the University of Chicago Law School to help me obtain 501(c)(3) status for my company (now the

Center), which would enable it to obtain charitable donations without tax liability either for me or my Center or for the donors; their efforts are described immediately after this introduction concludes.

At times I've wondered whether I really need donations. But with the growth of the company into the Center I think I do, and anyway the process of obtaining 501(c)(3) status has gone so far—is so close to completion—that I have no real alternative to the Center's being classified as a 501(c)(3). Above all I'm confident that the donations enabled by the 501(c)(3) classification will enhance the Center's ability to help pro se's—which is the goal. We have helped many pro se's, but only a small percentage. There are reliably believed to be at least a million pro se's in the United States, probably more, many of whom don't realize they can obtain assistance in obtaining the protection of the law. I will continue trying to prioritize those pro se needs that are most urgent yet are receiving little attention.

An issue that cannot be escaped is shielding the Center's personnel from malpractice liability; to that end—and confirming the need for additional assets—I shall endeavor to use some of the donations received by the Center to finance the purchase of malpractice insurance for the Center's members.

Another constructive use of donations will be financing occasional conferences in the Center's imposing downtown Chicago offices and meeting rooms on the fiftieth floor of 227 West Chicago Street that have been generously lent to us by Andrew Rosenfield; and we may also be holding conferences in other parts of the Center's widening geographical domain.

I have not yet mentioned the Center's board of directors. I have appointed its members (of whom Mr. Rosenfield is one), including the board chairman—the prominent New York financier Selvyn Seidel—and I expect donations from a number of them. But donations to one side, I regard the board as a consultative rather than a governing body. The Center remains under my control; I am its founder and president, my power over it being equivalent to that of the majority shareholder in a conventional firm. But I respect the important advice that I have received and expect to continue to receive from Mr. Seidel as chairman of the board; and I welcome criticism as well as advice from the board—though not governance of the Center by the board: for the number of cooks would be bound to spoil the broth.

The bylaws of the Center will be drafted to ensure that as President of the Center I will retain day-to-day decision making and operational management of it—but with one significant qualification: I have asked one of the outstanding members of my company, Brian Vukadinovich, and he has agreed, to be the executive director of the Center. All phone calls, emails, letters, and miscellaneous documents that heretofore have been to me should now be sent to Mr. Vukadinovich, who will forward them to me if he thinks me likely to be able to contribute to his response to the sender.

Finally, let me reiterate what I said recently in one of my books: I will not accept even a single penny for my work in administering the Center. That work is a labor of love.

Changing the Subject—Not for the Last Time

The company will be registered by the Illinois Attorney General; that is a prerequisite to my being allowed to solicit donations to it. But that is just the beginning. The bureaucratic details required to establish a company such as mine are formidable, indeed mind boggling, but it is something the readers of this book should be familiar with. I want to thank the efforts of Professor David Zarfes of the University of Chicago Law School, who presides over the University of Chicago Kirkland & Ellis Corporate Lab, and his students, notably but not only Phil Acevedo and Brian Crush, who along with Bruce R. Hopkins, a Kansas City lawyer and professor at the University of Kansas Law School who specializes in nonprofit organizations, of which Justice for Pro Se's [as it was still called when this section of the book was written] is one, are responsible for the administrative measures required to establish my company, which I now list; the words are Brian Crush's:

(1) Having submitted the incorporation documents for Justice for Pro Se's, we are waiting for the documents to be filed with the Illinois secretary of state and for the state to send us a file number for your company. We expect to receive it in the next 4 days, and will keep in touch with you and Theresa Yuan (the head of my [Posner's] research staff at the University of Chicago Law school) if we hear of any delays from the state. Processing Time: 4 days from now (approx).

(2) Once we receive this, we can apply for and receive a tax ID number for Justice for Pro Se's. Processing Time: 1 hour (once step 1 is complete).

(3) With these two steps completed, you [Posner] can open a bank account. Time: 1-2 hours (once steps 1-2 are complete).

(4) We are drafting the paperwork for the Illinois Attorney General and will submit it as soon as steps 1 and 2 are completed. Processing Time: 1-2 weeks (once the steps are complete).

(5) At this point in time you can accept donations, but see "part 5" below for the steps you need to take to do this.

(6) Submitting the IRS 501c3 application (form 1023): Phil Acevedo, another law student working for Professor Zarfes, and I [i.e., Brian Crush] are working on this form now but will not be able to complete it until steps 1 and 2 are complete (and again, we are waiting to hear from the state on the filed articles before step 1 is complete). We will need approximately a week to complete the form once steps 1 and 2 are complete and probably another week to run the paperwork by Bruce Hopkins and incorporate any edits or suggestions he may have. Once submitted, the IRS needs approximately 6 months (or more) to approve the paperwork. Processing Time: 2 weeks (once steps 1-2 are complete) for us to complete the paperwork, 6 months for IRS approval.

Details: what steps we've taken, and what we still need to do:

Part 1: Incorporation

We filled out the Illinois Articles of Incorporation for Justice for Pro Se's and have sent them to be processed. Because of the name change from Team Posner to Justice for Pro Se's there has been a delay in the processing, but we expect to get a confirmation of the filed articles from the state in the next 4 days. We need a copy of the filed articles of incorporation before we can proceed with submitting the documents below (the paperwork for each of the steps below require what is called a "file number" from the filed articles)--that said, we are drafting these documents now so they will be ready to send as soon as possible, but we need this file number before we can submit them.

Wolters Kluwer charges the fee to process the incorporation paperwork (including the fee to the secretary of state), provides annual report reminders to your team, and creates a Registered Agent for your company. Wolters is the parent company of CT Corporation—the service provider we discussed that will act as your company's Registered Agent. The fee pays for the incorporation of your company as well as establishing a registered agent for your company moving forward. Theresa Yuan is copied on the receipt for this charge and I am happy to email you a copy as well.

Part 2: A Tax ID

The IRS requires all businesses to have a Tax Identification Number (called an EIN, "Employer Identification Number"). This number is what you use to file the company's annual tax returns and is required to open bank accounts, pay employees (or independent contractors) and, generally, conduct business. There is no fee to get an EIN from the IRS, but the IRS does need your social security number. This process takes only 20 minutes to complete online and we can do this step the day we receive the filed incorporation documents.

Part 3: Opening a Bank Account

Once the two steps above are completed, you will be able to open a bank account. As we discussed on Monday, you may open an account in the name of the company at any bank of your choosing. We will provide you with all the paperwork needed to open the bank account and give a blueprint of the account process. Once the account is open, your company can accept deposits (any check written to Justice for Pro Se's) and make payments.

Part 4: Registering with the Illinois Attorney General

The state requires nonprofits to register themselves before soliciting donations. There are two forms that we need to submit to the Attorney General. We are drafting these forms now and will have them ready to go as soon as we get the incorporation documents back from the state and process the Tax ID (steps 1 and 2). This step requires a $15 fee to be paid to the Illinois Attorney General by check. We can coordinate with Theresa on getting your signature for these forms and picking up a check. Phil Acevedo will be able to physically submit these forms to the Attorney General. We expect this step to take no less than 5 days after we receive the incorporation documents.

Part 5: Accepting Donations

As we discussed on Monday, once these steps are completed above, you will technically be able to solicit donations even though your 501(c)(3) application has not yet been approved. Again, Justice for Pro Se's is not restricted from requesting or taking donation checks from your donors, but you will need to disclose to your donors that your 501c3 application is still pending and that your donors will not be able to deduct their donations until you receive the approval from the IRS.

INTRODUCTION – 15 –

Part 6: Filling and Submitting the IRS 501c3 Application (called the Form 1023)

This application gives your company the tax deductible status that will allow your donors to deduct their donations to Justice for Pro Se's. This process typically (and unfortunately) takes six months or more, because the IRS is quite slow in processing these applications. We are unable to submit this application until steps 1-2 are completed, but Phil and I (and the rest of our team) are preparing the application now in anticipation of submitting it to the IRS as soon as we can. Late yesterday evening Pam McKinney and Bruce Hopkins also contacted us to provide their support and double check the 1023 application before we submit it. We will work with Bruce to ensure that the application meets his approval before submitting it to the IRS. As I mentioned above, we do need this application to be approved before your donors can deduct their donations to Justice for Pro Se's. But they can make donations sooner; they will simply deduct their donations on their own tax forms after Justice for Pro Se's receives approval of this 1023 application. Lastly, there is a fee associated with this application, and it varies based on the gross receipts (the amount of money Justice for Pro Se's receives) within a year. We will stay in touch with you and Theresa regarding which fee will need to be paid (at a very high level, if the gross receipts are less than $50,000 annually the company pays a $275 fee, if it's greater than $50,000 the fee is $600).

Part 7: Miscellaneous filings

Justice for Pro Se's will also apply for an Illinois Revenue ID (a state taxpayer ID) as well as obtain Illinois state sales tax exemption status. These steps are not necessary to the above and we can complete them after we file the Form 1023. As with the IRS, the State also generates Employer ID numbers for tax filing purposes. In order to file State returns, you will need to generate an ID number. The Illinois Department of Revenue's website has instructions and online applications for receiving an Illinois Revenue ID.

Lastly, nonprofits qualify for State sales-tax exemptions. The Department of Revenue offers information and applications on its website. These applications are not necessary to achieve 501(c)(3) status, but you may be interested in examining both further. The Corporate Lab is happy to assist with filing for both.

The students' role in collecting and applying the voluminous legal regulations applicable to my company is well illustrated in a memo that they sent me (Richard Posner) several weeks ago written by Brian Crush that I wish to share with my readers. Here it is:

> Thank you for emailing us your updated memorandum. Per your earlier conversation with Phil [Acevedo], we will set up your company as a nonprofit corporation in the more simplified, scaled back approach as a single entity. We will not form the more complicated, two-company approach discussed in our group's earlier presentation that we offered you in November. As your company is not going to be offering legal advice or providing legal representation [but its members are—RAP], we agree that this makes very good sense.
>
> It also appears that your new year is off to a great start; congratulations on your case with Mr. Bond, and best of luck assisting him on his appeal to the Fourth Federal Circuit. In an abundance of caution we wanted to inquire whether you have or need to secure attorney malpractice insurance, if you are representing him in an attorney capacity. I (Posner) have written, and submitted to the court, a brief supportive of Bond's appeal, but I don't regard myself as representing him; he largely is representing himself, but has assistance from an excellent D.C. lawyer (and member of my firm) named Matthew Dowd.

Introduction

Our next action items are: (1) to file with the Illinois secretary of state, (2) to appoint a registered agent, and (3) to request a tax ID number for the company with the IRS. After these three are established, then we can (4) register with the attorney general and (5) begin the Form 1023 IRS nonprofit application. The fee charged by the Secretary of State is $75 (plus a small credit card transaction fee). Can we telephone you to obtain a credit card number from you to file the articles of incorporation? Please suggest any convenient times for us to contact you. Any time is fine (Posner).

We will use CT Corporation to act as your company's registered agent. A registered agency is a person or agency that a company appoints to receive official notices on the company's behalf. It includes service of process, correspondence with the state, and notifications of state and federal taxes due. CT's fee is $279 and we can register it online. CT will forward notices to your company for renewing its registered agent service as well as for filing annual reports with the Illinois Secretary of State. When your office receives these (which probably be in every December, starting in 2018) you may forward them to David Zarfes and Josh Avratin here at the law school and they can assist with the registered-agent renewal as well as the annual report.

Justice for Pro Se's will be your official registered business name with the state.

The articles of incorporation will also list the initial board of directors as we understand them: Richard A. Posner, Andrew Rosenfield, Selvyn Seidel, Ashley Keller, and George Dowd. Can you please confirm (yes) that these individuals are aware and have agreed to be listed as the initial board of directors for your company? The board can modify the directors at any time; this is simply for the initial registration with the state.

Once the secretary of state confirms registration we will get a Tax ID number. Armed with these two documents (the filed articles and the tax ID) you may open a bank account. Does Mr. Rosenfield's team at 227 W. Monroe (either an office manager or the mailroom) know that your company may occasionally receive mail in our office suite at 227 West Monroe? But most of the company's written and oral communications should be made either to Judge Posner's home phone in the case of oral communications or in the case of written communications his email address (rposner62@gmail.com) or street address (1222 East 56th Street, Chicago, Illinois 60637), or to Theresa Yuan's office phone number (773-702-9608) at the University of Chicago Law School.

Once the company is established, we will file it with the Illinois Attorney General; this registration is necessary to be allowed to solicit donations. The registration fee is $15.

Lastly, we enjoyed reading your most recent memo; the material in it will work well for your 1023 application with the IRS (which will give your company nonprofit approval so that you can have donors deduct their donations to your company). If you would like to add Phillip Acevedo and Brian Crush as consultants (yes), we will be happy to continue to offer whatever support and resources we can here at the Law School. Phil also contacted your research assistant Theresa about securing information for your 1023 application with IRS. We will work with her to ensure that we receive the necessary information to get your company's approval with the IRS as quickly as possible. She's excellent!

Thanks again, Dick, let us know if you have any questions. Phil or I can call you whenever is most convenient to receive your credit card information so as to be able to pay the fees to the state and to CT Corporation. We will also look into trademarking the company name "Justice for Pro Se's."

INTRODUCTION — 19 —

For completeness I (Posner) wish to note further remarks by Brian Crush, these arising from some pointers I received recently from Kate Groninger—a neighbor of mine who happens to be an expert on ethical standards and fiscal transparency in British and American museums, who has spoken at international museum conferences, published in museum journals, and worked in the U.S. museum industry, and with whom I had discussed my company briefly, deriving from her points that I thought might be relevant to Brian Crush's completing the formalities pertaining to the organization of my company.

The points that Ms. Groninger made were first that the articles of incorporation must include language required by the IRS to later secure the 501(c)(3) tax exemption, that they may also be required to include that specific verbiage in the organization's Bylaws, and that the following information from the Illinois Secretary of State's office should be of help: https://www.cyberdriveillinois.com/publications/pdf_/c165.pdf. Next she said that if my organization expects to have annual gross receipts under $50,000 at the outset [as it does], I may apply for tax-exempt status using the Form 1023-EZ application rather than the more complex/longer Form 1023; the benefit is that I won't have to wait 9+ months from the date of filing to obtain my 501(c)(3) status—only 3 months.

I asked Brian Crush what he thought of Ms. Groninger's suggestions. He responded positively, saying: Yes, these are good points—what your neighbor recommended in Point 1 is similar to what Bruce Hopkins recommended over the phone on Saturday. Continuing, Brian said that Phil Acevedo and he had reviewed the link that I had sent him a day earlier—https://www.cyberdriveillinois.com/publications/pdf_publications/c165.pdf—which incorporated material they had sent me last November! Continuing, Brian noted that my neighbor had also mentioned specific verbiage to be included in the articles of incorporation as well as in the company's bylaws. The Word document that you (that is, I) reviewed on Tuesday (I Brian reattach it here) has much of that specific verbiage that your neighbor is implying.

Before we submit your 501c3 application, your company will likely need a set of bylaws as well. I will speak with Phil [Acevedo] to get his recommendations on using the language in your handbook for the bylaws.

Continuing, Brian Crush addressed Groninger point 2, regarding form 1023-EZ. Phil and I [this of course is Crush speaking] reviewed this as well a few weeks ago and we think this is an excellent, faster way for your company to receive 501c3 status. However, the current draft of your budget (Theresa and Phil have communicated with regard to your company's budget for this year—I attach the current draft to this email) is at this point in time higher than $50,000. The IRS considers in-kind donations (including Mr. Rosenfield's office space) as well as cash donations to be part of your company's gross receipts for the year. If your company receives more than $50,000 in annual donations, the IRS requires that you fill out the regular 1023 application—the longer form with the longer processing time.

I see, Crush said, your (meaning my) note that your company does not intend to receive more than $50,000 this year. If so, the 1023-EZ is indeed an excellent option for payment, but I believe we will need to assure the IRS that your company will not receive donations in excess of $50,000.

I [Posner] responded rather feebly to Crush, as follows: "Two things, Brian. First, I have no idea how much money my firm will receive this year, but I expect it to exceed $50,000. The suite of offices that we received from Andrew Rosenfield on the 50th floor of 227 West Monroe Street is undoubtedly worth much more than that, and it was received this year—that is, after Jan. 1, 2018. I don't recall my note to the contrary that you mention, but it is out of date.

About by-laws I know nothing. I don't know what function they perform, and I don't know whether they are mandatory or optional; of course only if they're optional would there be grounds for my deciding not to have them.

This response elicited the following further remarks from Brian Crush:

"Dick, may I please clarify your response to this email? Do you expect your company's gross receipts to exceed $50,000 this year? The current amount of gifted office space on your budget is $80,000, and the total amount of expected donations (including in-kind donations) $101,200. The budget we received currently reflects this number but can be modified to match your expected donations and expenditures. We will continue to work on the Form 1023 with this budget, but we are happy to modify it to suit your company's budgetary plans. I will connect with Phil on the first of next week regarding the by-laws. Most of them are, like the detailed articles of incorporation, standard legalese regarding the operation of the company. Bruce Hopkins may have some valuable feedback on the by-laws as well. I will ask him for his input at the beginning of next week and follow up with him regarding review of the articles of incorporation."

And me again: Brian, I'm not sure about all the numbers. I am not planning on having an office manager. The head of my research team, currently Theresa Yuan, can easily double as office manager; likewise her successor when Theresa leaves at the end of this school year. I don't think there will be any office rent. Neither Theresa nor I are charged rent for her office. I don't pay rent for any use by me of the law school and its parking lot, or for my very occasional use of the suite of offices and meeting rooms on the 50th floor of 227 West Monroe, the suite given me by Andrew Rosenfield.

On March 1 I received a further communication from Brian Crush, again which I quote:

"You do not have any barriers at this point to discussing with your donors solicitation. You are welcome to begin the discussions with Selvyn Seidel and your other donors. We have been meticulous with your paperwork in order to ensure that your company receives its 501(c)(3) status and does so quickly. If your articles of incorporation or IRS applications do not meet the specific language that the IRS requires, as Bruce Hopkins explained, your company may be subject to additional review by the agency, which could delay your donors from deducting their donations to Justice for Pro Se's.

"If you follow the steps that Phil [Acevedo] and I outlined in our memo to you (check step 4), and disclose the 501(c)(3) status of your company (that it does not yet have 501(c)(3) and until it does, your donors will not be able to deduct their donations to Justice for Pro Se's) then you can begin discussing donations with your donors now.

"By next Friday, March 9, Law School finals will be over for the winter quarter. We will be able to complete the Attorney General filing shortly thereafter so that you can take donation checks. Until we can file this paperwork you cannot accept checks from your donors (but you are welcome to discuss). I expect to complete this in approximately 2.5 weeks and will remain in contact if we foresee any further delays. Again, we only heard from Bruce yesterday afternoon with his recommended language to include in the amended articles of incorporation. We will adapt these provisions and complete the paperwork as soon as the finals period is over.

"Feel free to discuss possible donations with your donors now. Over the next 2.5 weeks, once our finals for the winter quarter are complete, we can provide you with paperwork for opening a bank account, and get you and Theresa the attorney general forms for you to sign."

I (Posner speaking) thank Phil and Brian for their help getting my company set up, but I also wish to thank Theresa Yuan, the brilliant head of my superb seven-member research staff at the University of Chicago Law School: Makar Gevorkian, Steven Hazel, Jesse Hogin, John McAdams, Benjamin Meyer, Samuel Taxy, and Danielle York, for the valuable contributions they have made to my project. I further wish to acknowledge the contribution of the earlier mentioned Bruce R. Hopkins, a professor at the University of Kansas, the author of a major work on tax-exempt organizations (of which my company is one) called *The Law of Tax-Exempt Organizations* (11th ed. 2015). Professor Hopkins has advised me on ways (all lawful of course) of sparing Justice for Pro Se's from having to pay taxes. As explained by Brian Crush, "While the articles we drafted before meeting Bruce are compliant with the state of Illinois, based on our conversation with Bruce this morning, by including the articles with a greater level of granularity about the company's purpose and charitable nature, we will best set your company to get it approved for 501c3 status."

But now I want to dispel other possible confusion by emphasizing that my company is not a law firm; it is an organization devoted to assisting pro se's and other individuals and firms that need, but cannot afford or don't know how to utilize, legal assistance or guidance. The company includes lawyers among its members, but they are in the nature of volunteer helpers; they are not employees. Moreover the company's volunteer helpers also include advisors who are not members of any bar and indeed may not have attended law school, as well as consultants and a board of directors.

As yet the company has *no* employees, and the only employees it *will* have will be members of its office staff, which will operate out of offices at the University of Chicago Law School and possibly out of the suite of offices on the 50th floor of 227 West Monroe St. in downtown Chicago mentioned by Brian Crush—a suite generously gifted to Justice for Pro Se's by Andrew Rosenfield, a high-ranking business lawyer and financier involved in such companies as Guggenheim Partners and the

TGG Group. He is also a senior lecturer at the University of Chicago Law School, a member of my board of directors—and a former student of mine at the Law School when I was a professor there in the 1970s. (I am still a member of the law school faculty, but only part time.)

The downtown office suite will be available to company members who are not part of the office staff; indeed they are far more numerous. The suite is very elegant and also has spectacular views of the city from its large windows, consists both of offices, each equipped with a computer and a monitor, and meeting rooms; and a secretarial staff. I imagine that both company members who work in Chicago and members who visit Chicago from time to time will take advantage of their access to the suite.

There are many names in this book: of members of my company, of my former law clerks (some of them actual or potential members), of other lawyers and law firms, scattered around the country—lawyers and law firms with whom and with which I hope to work, including law firms from which it may be possible to obtain recruits for my company. Among other pertinent names are those of potential consultants and of members of my company's board of directors, along with names of research and office staff. Unfortunately it is not feasible for me to speak to all potential members of the company, whether in person or by phone. (Hence my need for an executive director, who as I said will be Brian Vukadinovich.) For the time being my direct communications are largely confined to pro se's seeking assistance, to lawyers and legal advisors working with or prepared to work with pro se's, and to potential consultants and board directors. But I hope that this book will function as a substitute for face-to-face communication, at least for a time, in this the developmental stage of what I hope will become in fairly short order a major enterprise. In addition, I will continue to issue frequent memoranda (of which this book is the culmination of those issued to date) to the members of my company and to potential allies.

Moving On

All or at least most of my volunteer helpers, both lawyers and nonlawyers, have as a condition of membership in the company agreed to devote some of their time to helping pro se's referred to them by me or other members of the company (again not employees—volunteer helpers!). The company is thus essentially a cooperative as distinct from a conventional corporation.

Both solely owned and solely led by me, at this writing the company is staffed by a total of 63 lawyers and nonlawyer advisors plus one consultant (Jennifer Nou) (but I am hoping that more consultants are on the way—see below), in 26 states and the District of Columbia, plus my 7-person law school research team, its director Theresa Yuan, and me—so a total of 70 members of my company, to which I'm hoping soon to add, as explained on pages 31 to 36 of this book, 9 more consultants and a 12-member board of directors, which would boost the company's total staff to 91. I hope also to attract donors as soon as my company is designated a 501(c)(3) nonprofit organization because donations to a 501(c)(3) are not taxed either to the donors or to the recipient company. I am organizing a board of directors to help manage my company; I expect also to receive donations from at least some of them. I envisage a board of nine or ten members with diverse backgrounds and interests. The board will meet periodically at the company's meeting rooms on the 50th floor of 227 West Monroe Street in downtown Chicago. I will have videoconference equipment installed so that any member of the board who would find it inconvenient because of distance or other obligations to attend in person can attend by Skype, phone, or other modes of communication.

Finally, as I'll be pointing out shortly, I am in the process of expanding the company's activities to the remaining U.S. states and eventually to other U.S. possessions as well, such as Puerto

Rico and Guam, an expansion that will further enlarge my staff of lawyers and of nonlawyer legal advisors.

And speaking of myself for a moment more, I hope that in providing legal guidance to pro se's my company members will not be afraid to deploy the heresies correctly ascribed to me by the distinguished New York lawyer Daniel J. Kornstein in the *New York Law Journal* of October 3, 2017, a month after my retirement from the Seventh Circuit Court of Appeals. Mr. Kornstein quoted me as saying that "I pay very little attention to legal rules, statutes, constitutional provisions. A case is just a dispute. The first thing you do is ask yourself—forget about the law—what is a sensible resolution of this dispute." Kornstein went on to flatter me by saying that "Posner may be doing what Oliver Wendell Holmes did 136 years ago in his book The Common Law," where he famously said: "The life of the law has not been logic, it has been experience. The felt necessities of the time, the prevalent moral and political theories, intuitions of public policy avowed or unconscious, even the prejudices which judges share with their fellow-men, have a good more to do than the syllogism in determining the rules by which men should be governed.... Able and experienced judges know too much to sacrifice good sense to a syllogism." Kornstein remarks that both Holmes and Posner "are rejecting an abstract notion of the law. Instead they favor a pragmatic, problem-solving, dispute-resolving approach. Drop the mask, they are saying. Don't think of law as a disembodied, transcendental concept. Consider it a tool for deciding disputes fairly. Focus on the realities of life.... Posner's recent eye-catching and provocative comments may bring us up short, but they are in good company and part of an honorable tradition. He doesn't really mean we should 'forget' about the law, but that we should not make a fetish of it at the expense of its real-world impact."

Kornstein's article echoed to a degree an earlier article, by former *New York Times* columnist Emily Bazelon—"Better Judgment," *New York Times Sunday Magazine*, June 21, 2015,

p. MM46—in which she called me "a self-defined pragmatist [who] is probably Holmes's closest intellectual heir today. ... For years, Posner has argued that judges should be less concerned about theories or past precedent and 'more open to the facts. Most judges start with the old stuff,' he said, 'But they should ask themselves, given modern conditions, what is the right result? When I get a new case, I ask myself, 'What is the common-sense solution here?'"

There is a fainter, but more amusing echo. Harry Hopkins was and apparently still is widely regarded as having been President Franklin Delano Roosevelt's most influential advisor before and during World War II because of his unrivaled influence on and access to the President. At the same time it was said of him by another influential bureaucrat in the Roosevelt administration that he "was bound by no preconceived notions, no legal inhibitions, and absolutely no respect for tradition." Hey, that's me!

Coming to the Present

Pro se's are in a difficult position, not only because most of them can't afford lawyers and the rest don't have lawyers, but also and perhaps more importantly because of widespread judicial hostility to them; they are thought by many judges unworthy of the attention of the judiciary. As explained in detail in my two books mentioned at the outset of this book, I retired from my court last September because of my distress at the summary fashion in which the court disposed of pro se appeals—disposed of them even when they had merit.

This problem, which I vow to make every effort through my firm to solve, is discussed in a recent article by Sonja Ebron published on the website of Courtroom5, the name of the company of which she is co-owner with Debra Slone. The title of the article is "It Takes an Unbiased Judge to Call Out Judicial Bias," which points out that in retiring from the Seventh Circuit

Court of Appeals I (the "unbiased judge" to whom she's referring) accused the court of funneling pro se appeals to staff lawyers, to be summarily dismissed over trivial technical issues, and said that his [i.e., my] colleagues refused to let him [i.e. me] work with staff lawyers on their recommendations." Ms. Ebron goes on to note that "judicial bias is the biggest threat to justice, and there's nothing to help judges grapple with that." She sensibly suggests that "the best way to combat judicial bias is to surpass the judge's expectations. File the right documents and make the right arguments in court. This is not impossible when the expectations are so low. Follow these guidelines: (1.) Include in your filings only the information the court needs to understand your legal position. Don't argue the case before trial. (2.) Support your case with solid legal research, and pepper your arguments with relevant citations to legal authority. (3.) File pleadings and motions that follow standard legal formatting. Don't write letters to the judge." Her advice is excellent, and Justice for Pro Se's will work closely with Ms. Ebron's company to assist pro se's. I discuss our prospective relations with her company at greater length later in this book.

Our Credo

We as a team can and I hope will accomplish more for the pro se community than has ever been done before. We have a virtually infinite number of choices of how to make a difference. The most important threshold issues are how best to spend our finite time and how to organize an effective institution.

First and foremost is our commitment to help pro se individuals, in whatever respects their legitimate needs dictate, to the extent we're able. The members of my company have each made that choice, and the pro se world is the fortunate beneficiary of the choice.

Second we need to identify who and what deserve our help the most, and establish priorities on the basis of what we now know and re-examine those priorities after we have more experience. We will focus on assisting pro se individuals (of course including pro se women, though they are far fewer than pro se men) who have difficulties in the criminal arena in particular state courts and in the civil arena in particular state and federal courts. We'll include in our program the education and training of pro se individuals and also of lawyers and non-lawyer legal advisers, an important component of our company. We will doubtless want to coordinate with, and possibly align with, selected other organizations, such as other pro se organizations, such as Courtroom5, legal aid organizations, translators, law schools, and pro bono lawyers' law firms. Just as "pro se" is Latin for "for yourself," "pro bono" is Latin for "for the good," and is a term given lawyers who represent pro se's without seeking compensation.

Monitoring the Company

At the same time we need to continue working to create the structure and organization that we need to work within. We want an institution, one that endures. After a year or two, we should take stock of things, and adjust as needed and possible. But the process of adjustment has now begun. Brian Vukadinovich, one of the brightest stars in our firmament and mentioned and quoted frequently in this book, has at my urging agreed to share with me the difficult, time-consuming, but essential task of monitoring the activities, present and prospective, of our company in every state in which it is represented. The number of our representatives, and the number of states, will grow. But that is for the future; for now the acute need is for adequate monitoring of our existing representatives.

The newly appointed Regional Directors, discussed later in the book, will do much of the monitoring; this book lists the directors and the territories constituting the region of each of them. But there must be some central direction as well. And under my new regime Mr. Vukadinovich and I will be sharing responsibility for that direction, responsibility that will include monitoring the activity of our representatives in each state (including the Regional Directors), relating to the local law firms and at times recruiting lawyers in those firms to join Justice for Pro Se's whether on a part-time or a full-time basis, learning as much as possible about the pro se's in the state, and sharing information with other pro bono organizations in the state.

Mr. Vukadinovich and I will divide responsibility for rhe regions as follows. He will be responsible for the two regions of which he is already the director—Indiana, and Illinois south of Chicago—plus Jonathan Zell's region, which consists of Ohio, Michigan, Kentucky, and West Virginia; plus Matthew Dowd's region, which encompasses the District of Columbia, Maryland, Virginia, North Carolina, and South Carolina; and last, lawyer Alan Popkin's region, which is Missouri. I will be responsible for the remaining regions.

Mr. Vukadinovich has expressed to me justified concern about the dearth of regions of our company in the nation's western states. I would very much like to have a region consisting of California, Nevada, Oregon, Washington, Utah, Arizona, New Mexico, and possibly others. I'll call that group of states a "prospective" region and write to lawyers or law firms in the region who may be interested in becoming Regional Directors for Justice for Pro Se's. It would be great to have regional authority in those states, as there are doubtless many pro se's needing help in them (not limited to California), and there are many good law schools in them producing lawyers who might wish to unite with my company and perhaps become Regional Directors.

I am confident that the measures I have described, given the contribution that Mr. Vukadinovich will make, will constitute a giant step forward for our company. But it goes without saying that I invite your insights into and reactions to the new program. I would therefore appreciate any suggestions that the readers of this book may have for maximizing the impact of our company. We the members and managers of the company will consider such suggestions carefully and doubtless benefit greatly from that consideration.

And Where, By the Way, Do We Work?

At this writing the members of my company do not work at a single specified location, equivalent to the trading floor of a stock exchange. I work in my home office, with occasional visits to my law school research team and/or the team's director, Theresa Yuan; their workplaces are in the law school. The company's other members are scattered across a number of states plus the District of Columbia (which of course is not a state) — eventually, I am confident, the "scatter" of our personnel will embrace all fifty states plus federal enclaves that like the District of Columbia, Puerto Rico, Guam, and other territories are parts of the United States though they are not states.

But the locational situation is about to change as a consequence of the generous gift, mentioned earlier, of Mr. Rosenfield to my company of the very large, very modern set of offices and meeting rooms, replete with computers and monitors and secretarial staff, on the 50th floor of 227 West Monroe Street, Chicago. I expect some company members to relocate to the suite rather than remain scattered (as many now are) throughout Chicago and vicinity. As mentioned earlier, meetings of the board of directors will be held there. A further discussion of the board begins on page 31 and culminates on pages 34 to 36. The company will become more efficient as a result of its acquisition of so spacious, imposing, well maintained, and well located an office suite.

I had thought initially that I would need an office manager and research librarian in the 50th floor suite. But on reflection, and on observation of the extraordinary work of my chief research assistant, Theresa Yuan, I believe that a chief research assistant, if very carefully selected, is all that is needed. Ms. Yuan has demonstrated that a highly competent chief research assistant with seven or so law student researchers under his or her command can do everything that a chief research assistant, office manager, and research librarian need to be able to do: to wit

- Perform legal research
- Perform intake for all prisoners' and pro se's letters arriving at Justice for Pro Se's law school address.
- Direct the student research assistants to complete research tasks for intake (for example, looking up individual states' laws, checking on statutes of limitations, looking up sentencing rules and practices).
- Assign research projects to the student assistants on the basis of Posner's research interests and the company's needs (memos on, for example, legal ethics, sentencing, prisoners' rights, and trends in pro se litigation).
- Prepare a proposed budget for my company's soon to be incorporated status as a nonprofit corporation and maintain communication with the pertinent law school team, consisting of Professor David Zarfes and his brilliant students Phil Acevedo and Brian Crush, with regard to filling out and submitting correct forms and gathering necessary information. This program is well in tow.
- Maintain a website conveying essential information about the activities of Justice for Pro Se's.

- Mail letters to (or phone) pro se's asking for additional information, or rejecting their cases, based on Posner's instructions.
- Help me register for the Illinois bar and maintain my registration with the New York bar.
- Collect information about what each volunteer is doing for my company and maintain this information in a spreadsheet; also track assigned cases.
- Open the downtown office suite when Justice for Pro Se's volunteers are visiting and set up videoconferencing at the suite based on my or the company's needs, notably for board of directors meetings.

Intake Information Form

Cases come to Justice for Pro Se's in phone calls, emails, letters, or a website intake form. We ask pro se's and others seeking the assistance of company members to fill out this short intake information form and submit it with their request for assistance:

Name: _____

Address: _____

Telephone: _____

Email: _____

Please tell us what type of help you're requesting. Example (a): I need advice on how to proceed on my own, (b) I need a lawyer to represent me. What kind of a case are you involved in that you need help with? Civil case or criminal case? Please describe the issue(s) in the case as well as you can. Is the case currently in court? If so, please state which court, and the location and title of the case, including the case number. What is the name of the judge presiding over the case? What is the name(s) of the opposing lawyer(s)? What is the status of the case if it's already in formal litigation? Did you previously have an attorney? If so, what was his or here name and what was the reason he or she is no longer representing you in the case? And finally do you have evidence to support your claim? If so, please describe that evidence for us.

Company members working on intake for prison inmates (for as I said earlier about half of all pro se's are inmates) must be sure to obtain the following information from persons writing to or calling members (often Posner himself) for help: Sentence(s) and offense(s) for which the individuals are currently serving their term; any and all appeals they have filed in the past and their outcomes; any information related to ongoing litigation (they may explain in a letter why they believe they have a strong case). Each inmate should enclose copies of any transcripts, case documents, affidavits, etc. that bear on the case, plus the names of any lawyers or legal aid organizations they have contacted about the case and the responses they received from them. We'll decide which cases have sufficient merit to assign to pro bono lawyers or to non-lawyers. I'll contact those individuals whose cases are rejected, giving the reasons for the rejection, and I may also refer those individuals to other providers of legal assistance who may be able to help them.

It's obvious, but worth repeating: we cannot help a pro se without full knowledge of his needs, situation, capability, and prospects.

Let's Make My Company Nationwide!

At present, members of my company are found in the following 27 states (treating the District of Columbia as a state):

1.	California	15.	Minnesota
2.	Colorado	16.	Missouri
3.	Connecticut	17.	Nebraska
4.	Delaware	18.	Nevada
5.	District of Columbia	19.	New York
6.	Florida	20.	Ohio
7.	Georgia	21.	Rhode Island
8.	Idaho	22.	South Carolina
9.	Illinois	23.	Tennessee
10.	Indiana	24.	Texas
11.	Kentucky	25.	Vermont
12.	Maine	26.	Virginia
13.	Maryland	27.	Wisconsin
14.	Massachusetts		

That leaves 24 states, plus the nation's five overseas territories (American Samoa, Guam, the North Mariana Islands, Puerto Rico, and the United States Virgin Islands) — in none of which however my company has as yet any representatives. The 24 states are as follows:

1. Alabama
2. Alaska
3. Arizona
4. Arkansas
5. Hawaii
6. Iowa
7. Kansas
8. Louisiana
9. Michigan
10. Mississippi
11. Montana
12. New Hampshire
13. New Jersey
14. New Mexico
15. North Carolina
16. North Dakota
17. Oklahoma
18. Oregon
19. Pennsylvania
20. South Dakota
21. Utah
22. Washington
23. West Virginia
24. Wyoming

The states in which my company has representatives are shown in dark gray in the following map.

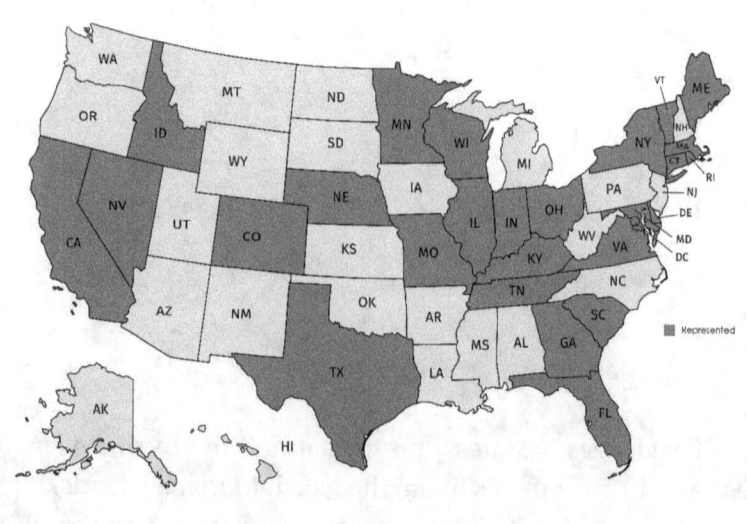

Let's get members of my company in all those other 24 states! To that end I am mailing this book to all my former law clerks except four (Daniel Klerman, Lawrence Lessig, Gregory Sidak, and Rebecca Stone) who have already joined or indicated their intention or willingness to join my company, and also mailing it to all the lawyers and law firms to whom or to which I previously sent solicitations in states and territories in which the company has as yet no representatives. I am hopeful that these mailings will get us significantly nearer the goal of having representatives in all the states plus the District of Columbia and eventually in the U.S. territories outside the Continental United States as well.

But I aim to achieve this expansion less by stationing members of my existing staff in these other states and territorial possessions than by inviting a select group of lawyers and other legal advisors active in a variety of U.S. states and territories to associate with my firm as volunteer affiliates willing, just like the members of my company, to devote some time to providing advice and other services to pro se's in their states or territories similar to the services that my company provides in the states in which it has staff. We'll assist the affiliates in a variety of ways, including advice, loan of staff, and financial assistance (eventually—at present the finances of the firm have not crystallized, though they will as soon as the firm is converted to a 501(c)(3) firm), in that way making my company a truly nationwide enterprise serving a very large number of pro se's and others in need of legal advice and assistance. It is worth noting in this connection that there are reliably believed to be literally millions of pro se's in the United States.

In considering affiliation with lawyers and other volunteer helpers in states and other areas in which I don't as yet have staff, I will consider the extent of the commitment of such affiliates to my company as evidenced for example by willingness to take on cases referred to them by us and to refer particular such cases to other lawyers or helpers in their state if unable to take on those cases themselves. I might say to them, "Would you be interested in joining my panel of pro bono lawyers? I am hoping to assign you any cases with merit that are in your state. And should you be unable to take on a particular case I hope you'll recommend one or two other good lawyers in your state who could take it on."

I need to emphasize the importance of feedback from the helpers to me. My objective is of course to help pro se's, but I have not required the members of my staff to help any specified *number* of pro se's per year. Moreover, none of the members has yet to tell me how many pro se's he or she has assisted in the past year or years. I can't criticize them for not having told me, because the company has been in existence for only a few months and I haven't yet told the members how often I want each one of them to report the number of pro se's that he or she has assisted in a given time period. I'll be happy to receive such information at any time, but I shall expect *at least* an *annual* report from each member of the company on the number of pro se's assisted by him or her in the previous year; and I would of course prefer more frequent feedback. This point is of course related to my earlier point about the monitoring of our company's representatives by Mr. Vukadinovich and me.

I should add that the assistance rendered to pro se's by company members needn't be courtroom presentation. It can be "ghostwriting" (explained later in this book); it can be teaching a pro se to be his own courtroom lawyer; it can be assisting a litigant who is not a pro se but needs the kind of assistance that members of my company can provide; it can be instruction found in a book or an article, a speech or an op ed.

But lately it's occurred to me that there is a more efficient method of obtaining feedback from members of my company than the one just described: and that is to designate each one of a set of members experienced in representing or otherwise assisting pro se's to be responsible for making monthly phone calls to members in a specified geographical area. Each caller will inquire what relations (assistance, rejection, whatever) the members in the geographical area assigned to the caller have had to pro se's in their designated area. The caller's questions might be particularized as follows, though these are my suggestions, not orders: how many pro bono cases did you handle this month? And for how many persons? How many of your hours did your cases consume? How did you get the cases—from lawyers, prisoners, judges? How many pro se cases did you turn down, and why?

From the reports of the callers and the fruits of the monitoring undertaken by Mr. Vukadinovich and me, I'll learn how successful the company is in performing its mission of assisting pro se's. Many, probably most, of the callers will be my Regional Directors, about whom more later.

I can further clarify my concern with feedback by noting a distinction between self and society. The members of my company are each of them separate, autonomous selves (or, if one prefers, souls). But they are also social beings, specifically members of my company. Subject to my division of responsibilities with Mr. Vukadinovich, I would very much like to hear not only from the "callers" described above but also from every member when (or not too long after) he or she assists a pro se; for that will enable me to evaluate the productivity of each member and hence of the company as a whole—and it will also enable needed financial assistance. As of today the finances of the company remain speculative, conjectural—one might even say spectral. That's about to change, however. As noted above, within a short time the company should be established as a 501(c)(3) corporation—a nonprofit organization financed by charitable contributions that are taxed neither to the corporation nor to its donors, provided that the corporation is itself either a religious or a charitable, rather than a profit-making, organization. Yet even after its conversion to a 501(c)(3) entity, the company will remain, as it is today, a nonprofit charitable organization. (Indeed 501(c)(3) companies are required to be nonprofit, charitable organizations.)

Anent feedback, a recent article by Maura Ewing, entitled "A Judicial Pact to Cut Court Costs for the Poor," https://www.heatlantic.com/politics/archive/2017/12/court-fines-north-carolina/548960/, is full of suggestions that can help in defining the roles of my company's members. Ms. Ewing explains that if you ("you" being a member of the company) are a pro bono lawyer (that is, you do not charge your client), then you don't have to worry about your client's impecuniousness. But you will not be reimbursed by my company for the expenses you incur in these cases; that is the nature of pro bono representation. In addition you'll have to maintain your own malpractice insurance if you think such insurance necessary. You may if you want, or if you feel obliged to, report your participation in my company to your law firm (if you are a member of a law firm). And you may count hours spent on cases that you've obtained from me toward your state bar's pro bono requirements.

To facilitate accurate record keeping, members of my company should provide either me or the chief of my research staff, Theresa Yuan (theresayuan@uchicago.edu), answers to the following questions:

If you are a lawyer:

> What is your preferred email address?
>
> What is a phone number at which potential clients, and members of my company, can reach you?
>
> How many hours a month can you devote to working on cases assigned by me?
>
> Where are you admitted to practice law? (Please include all federal appellate and district courts and state courts)

What types of case do you normally handle for your firm, or for yourself if you're in a firm? What kinds of case would you be interested in working on pro bono?

Do you have any other skills and interests that you'd like to contribute to my firm? (for example co-authoring briefs, writing reports, intake, etc.)

If you are a non-lawyer advisor but have extensive experience with litigation:

Can you teach litigants who do not require representation in court how they can best represent themselves in court?

What is your email address? What is you phone number? How many hours a month can you devote to working one-on-one with pro se's? Which state or federal courts are you most familiar to you?

Do you have any other skills and interests that you'd like to contribute to my company such as co-authoring briefs, writing reports, and handling intake?

If you're unable or unwilling to represent pro se's, are you willing to serve in an advisory capacity for case strategy, including overall direction of the company, intake, amicus curiae briefs, policy initiatives—in other words be a consultant (more on consulting and consultants below)?

How many hours a month can you devote to assignments by my company? And which of the following types of work would you be interested in: intake (already mentioned: evaluating claims for assistance by the company): consulting on individual cases; writing amicus curiae briefs, reports for publication, guides for pro se', or other types of document pertinent to my company's needs.

And bear in mind that you can donate non-legal services or funds to my company. If you do donate, may the company include your name on the website of Justice for Pro Se's as a donor? Would you like to be consulted about specific cases? What service or funds would you like to donate to Justice for Pro Se's?

Interruption: Listen Carefully!

As sole owner, I pledge not to accept even a single penny from the company, whether as compensation, payback, incentive pay, reward, or otherwise characterized, and whether the company is in its present or its soon to be 501(c)(3) form. But though sole owner, I intend to share management of the company with a board of directors that will be constituted soon and is discussed below. A major function of the directors will be to make, and solicit others to make, substantial donations to the company.

Consultants

I have my first consultant—Jennifer Nou, a professor at the University of Chicago Law School and formerly a law clerk first to me and then to Supreme Court Justice Breyer; afterward she became the principal assistant to Harvard Professor Cass Sunstein when he was the Administrator of the White House Office of Information and Regulatory Affairs in the Obama administration. And so I need to explain the difference between consulting and the actual handling of a case, whether inside or outside a courtroom and whether by a lawyer, including a "ghostwriter" (a lawyer who drafts documents or provides other assistance to a pro se but does not make an appearance in the case), or by a highly knowledgeable nonlawyer advisor such as Brian Vukadinovich, who can train a pro se to be his or her own courtroom lawyer. By a consultant I mean a knowledgeable person, not necessarily a lawyer, who provides helpful analysis and information to a pro se litigant or a litigant's lawyer or advisor but does not represent the litigant. It is a role I play constantly, as I am a frequent recipient of inquiries from pro se's.

There will be no fixed work requirement for consultants. Consulting is not their primary work and must therefore be fitted into their regular work schedules. I intend to compensate the consultants for their contributions to the company.

I want to break away from consultants and introduce the reader to an unconventional but in my opinion extremely valuable and important method of assisting pro se's in litigation. The method is a manual for teaching pro se's how to be their own courtroom lawyers. Here is the manual, preceded by a brief introduction by me:

Brian Vukadinovich, a very major member of my company as I have said, came to my attention when I learned that, without legal representation and with no background of legal training or knowledge, he had won a $203,000 judgment in a civil jury trial that pitted him, the plaintiff, against the public school board that had fired him from his job as a high school teacher and basketball coach. Shortly afterward he drafted the manual, still very much in use; I quote from the short introduction that I wrote for it, and then I quote the manual itself. The manual is proof positive that an intelligent person can be trained, or train himself, to be his own courtroom lawyer and do better in court representing himself than if he had a lawyer:

[My introduction continued]: Mr. Vukadinovich recently drafted a very fine pro se manual which my firm will use: Here is his lucid introduction to his manual, followed by the manual itself; you will notice that, critically, the manual aims to teach pro se's to represent themselves rather than seek representation by a lawyer. It is a notable achievement.

The Vukadinovich Documents

This is a rough draft with some ideas for a pro se manual for your [Posner's] new firm. It is bare bones and certainly not a final product. I am sure your staff will want to make additions, deletions, adjustments, etc. There are of course a million things that could be discussed, but I tried to keep it to the main problem areas that pro se's have communicated to me in terms of the problem areas they have encountered in trying to represent themselves. I added in the trial preparation section at the end just for some general information about the pro se calls that I have received, none has made it to trial, but I went ahead and put a bit of trial information in there. To a person, their difficulties lie with dealing with summary judgment motions. That is the single biggest problem that all who have called me are experiencing. In my assessment of the conversations I have had, they generally didn't do adequate discovery leading up to the summary judgment motion, and didn't understand case law and how to apply them to the issues. After determining that their discovery was weak, some would ask if it was too late to undertake further discovery, during the pendency of the summary judgment process. These are just some thoughts from my perspective from talking with pro ses. In my opinion, major emphasis needs to be placed on learning how to conduct effective discovery in order to effectively combat summary judgment, and on learning at least some adequate research abilities to be able to effective cite case law to the arguments. Feel free to use the pro se manual in however way you would like. As I said, it is only bare bones, as I am sure your skilled staff will improve it tremendously, but I hope it can be of some help.

THE PRO SE MANUAL

INTRODUCTION

The purpose of this manual is to give you some helpful insight into the essential areas of the law that you will need to know to help prepare you to represent yourself in your case hopefully to a successful conclusion. Hopefully the information will help you better understand the obstacles you are likely to encounter and perhaps overcome with a better understanding of the principles that will be necessary to prosecute your case and to avoid dismissal of your case by potential motions to dismiss or motions for summary judgment that will in all likelihood be employed by defense attorneys. Under the law you have every right to represent yourself as the Judiciary Act of 1789 states "That in all courts of the United States, the parties may plead and manage their own causes personally".

DETERMINE ANY PREREQUISITES TO FILING SUIT

Depending on the state you live in or the nature of action you are pursuing, you may be required to first submit a notice of tort claim if your claim is a state claim against a state governmental agency. Be sure to research your state's particular laws with respect to time periods that your notice must be submitted in order that you don't unintentionally waive any of your legal rights for failure to timely submit a tort claims notice. If your claim involves discrimination in violation of a federal statute, then you must first file an EEOC charge in the office of the appropriate jurisdiction. Generally discrimination claims for violations of federal statutes require a discrimination charge to be filed with the Equal Employment Opportunity Commission (EEOC) within 180 days of the occurrence of the discriminatory act. Failure to timely file the discrimination charge with the EEOC could result in waiver of your right to seek redress for the discrimination claim(s) in a court of law. Once a discrimination charge is filed with the Equal Employment Opportunity Commission, your charge will be investigated and the EEOC will issue a finding if it finds cause, and if it is not able to issue a finding of cause based on the information it has been provided, it will issue a right to sue letter after it concludes its investigation giving you the right to file a lawsuit in a court of law. Once you are provided with a right to sue letter from the EEOC, you then have 90 days to file your lawsuit from the date that you receive your right to sue letter.

GET FAMILIAR WITH THE GOVERNING RULES OF COURT

It is very important to familiarize yourself with the governing rules of the court where you will be filing your cause of action. Many pro ses make the mistake of proceeding with their litigation without studying the governing rules of procedure and that can be very costly in terms of the fate of your case. Defense lawyers love to find technical flaws with a pro se's procedure and they look for any missteps that the pro se may make in not following the governing rules. Many times the failure to know and follow the rules of procedure result in a dismissal of a case. These dismissals can be avoided to a large degree simply by taking the time to familiarize yourself with the rules. That would include the state or federal rules of procedure, depending on which venue you are in, and also the local rules of the particular court you are in. If the case is in federal court, it would be the Federal Rules of Civil Procedure. If the case is in state court, you would need to research the rules of procedure from that particular state.

GET FAMILIAR WITH TERMS GENERALLY USED IN LITIGATION

You will run into many legal terms that you may have never heard of before, for example such as *"in limine"*, "voir dire",

"*Daubert* motions", "estoppel", and many others, and it is very important that you learn what those terms mean if and when they come up in your case. You can do this by obtaining a dictionary of legal terms or of course with an internet search.

PREPARING AND FILING THE COMPLAINT

The general rules of pleading are such that you must file a complaint stating a claim for relief. To adequately state a proper claim for relief the complaint must contain three essential elements:
1) a short plain state of the grounds for the court's jurisdiction, unless the court already has jurisdiction and the claim needs no new jurisdiction support;
2) a short and plain statement of the claim showing that the pleader is entitled to relief; and
3) a demand for the relief sought, which may include relief in the alternative or difference types of relief.

Be sure to look up the particular pleading laws in whatever venue you are filing your case. If you are filing in a state court, the laws vary from state to state and some states, such as Indiana for example, do not permit a dollar amount to be stated. Federal court complaints allow plaintiffs to state the dollar amount to which they are seeking in damages. If you desire a jury trial, you must state your jury demand within your complaint. If you are seeking redress in a federal court, federal courts are required to liberally construe your pleadings with less stringent standards under the decision of *Haines v. Kerner*, et al., 401 U.S. 519; (1972). It is important to state enough sufficient facts in your pro se complaint in order to withstand a motion to dismiss for failure to state a claim for relief. This will be one of the first things that that the defense attorney(s) will look for soon after your case is filed as defense attorney(s) routinely will try this tactic early on in the litigation if they see a possible opportunity with a flawed complaint.

DISCOVERY

Conducting effective discovery is a very crucial aspect of prosecuting your case in terms of obtaining information and evidence to prove your case and also to defend against any dispositive motions. If your cause of action is in a federal court, you should refer to the Federal Rules of Civil Procedure. If your cause of action is in a state court you should refer to the rules of court from that particular state. Rule 26(b)(1) of the Federal Rules of Civil Procedure states the discovery scope and limits as follows:

> Unless otherwise limited by court order, the scope of discovery is as follows: Parties may obtain discovery regarding nonprivileged matter that is relevant to any party's claim or defense and proportional to the needs of the case, considering the importance of the issues at stake in the action, the amount in controversy, the parties' resources, the importance of the discovery in resolving the issues, and whether the burden or expense of the proposed discovery outweighs its likely benefit. Information within this scope of discovery need not be admissible in evidence to be discoverable.

There are several avenues of discovery that you should get familiar with and utilize that can be very helpful:

Interrogatories, which are written questions that you can submit to any and all of the defendant(s) in your case that are to be answered under oath. Generally, the defendants will have thirty (30) days to respond to your interrogatories from the date they receive them.

Depositions, which are oral question you can ask of any of the defendant(s) in your case. While this is a very effective means of discovery, it can be expensive as you will have to employ a court reporter for this. If you are able to conduct effective depositions, you will in all likelihood be able to obtain information that will be very helpful in proving your case and also very helpful in responding to any motions for summary judgment that the defendants will likely file in your case.

Requests for Production are requests you can make to the defendants to produce documents and tangible things for your review that you can use to help prove your case and to respond against any motions for summary judgement that the defendants may file in an attempt to have your case dismissed without a trial.

Requests for Admissions are written requests that you can make to any and all of the defendants in your case for the defendant(s) to admit or deny certain facts and the genuineness of any described documents. Effective use of requests for admissions can be very helpful to prove your case and also to respond to any motions for summary judgment.

DISPOSITIVE MOTIONS

In most cases, and especially since you are proceeding pro se, you can expect the defendants to file some type of a dispositive motion in an effort to have your case dismissed without a trial. Usually this happens with a motion to dismiss for a technical reason of some kind or a motion for summary judgment where the defendants will argue that there is no genuine dispute as to any material fact and that the defendant is entitled to judgement as a matter of law. You must understand what a "fact" is in the eyes of the law; a "fact" can be a statement made or an action taken. And that "fact" has to be "material", something that matters, something of consequence to the issue. A "genuine dispute" is proven by contradictory or conflicting evidence. "Matter of law" are the components of a claim as defined by statutes and appellate court decisions. If your action is in federal court this rule would be found in Rule 56 of the Federal Rules of Civil Procedure. If you are in a state court you should research that state's summary judgment rules. This is a very critical aspect of your case that you should be well prepared to respond to because if you fail to file an adequate response to the defendant's motion for summary judgment, and the defendant's motion is granted, your case is over and you get no trial. You can of course appeal the decision to a court of appeal but it is always a good thing to be prepared to file a strong response and overcome a filing of a motion for summary judgment. You should be prepared to rebut the caselaws filed by the defendant and to submit caselaws that are favorable to your position. You need to learn how to research the caselaws relevant to the issues of your case for two substantial reasons, first, you need to cite supporting caselaws to convince the judge that the law is on your side on the issue, and secondly, the defense lawyer(s) will generally cite a multitude of cases to support the defendant's position. As a pro se, the defense lawyers will try to overwhelm you with the citation of an enormous amount of caselaws, many of which may not even be relevant to the case and calculated to just overwhelm you. You will need to know how to read and understand those caselaws in order that you can argue against their relevancy to the issues in your case. Many times cases that are cited by defendant's lawyers are actually helpful to your case as defense lawyers may only point to one or two sentences in the entire case and there many times are many areas of those cases that actually can be helpful to your position. But you must know how to read and properly apply the caselaws in order that you may make an intelligent argument to the court. You should be prepared to submit evidence in support of your response showing that there is a genuine dispute as to the material facts and that the defendant is not entitled to summary judgement as a matter of law. This is where your due diligence with how you conducted your discovery will be very helpful as you would be able to use the information and evidence you obtained in your discovery, i.e., interrogatories, depositions, requests for production, requests for admissions, etc., to help defeat the defendant's motion for summary judgment.

PREPARING FOR TRIAL

There will be a multitude of things you will have to do to prepare for trial which will be outlined by the court in an order controlling the case such as deadline dates for the filing of any pretrial motions such as dispositive motions, motions in limine, which are motions to prevent the opposing side from introducing certain items of information or evidence, proposed final pretrial order, contentions, stipulations of fact, exhibit list and witness list proposed jury instructions and your objections to the defendants' jury instructions, if the matter is going to be tried to a jury rather than a bench trial. Depending on your court's local rules, you will have to prepare voir dire questions, which are questions to be asked of potential jurors during jury selection. You will of course have to have copies of all of your exhibits, labeled, with a copy that you will introduce into evidence and a copy for the court and defense counsel. You should become familiar with how to do an effective opening and closing statement. You should become familiar with the rules of procedure for whatever court venue you are in, if a federal action, it will be the Federal Rules of Civil Procedure. If in state court, it will be that particular state's rules of procedure. In addition to becoming familiar with the rules of civil procedure you need to become knowledgeable with the rules of evidence in order that you will know how to get your evidence admitted at the trial. If it is a federal court action it will be the Federal Rules of Evidence, if a state court action you will need to research that particular state's rules of evidence. If you do not do adequate preparation and if you do not do your homework in becoming knowledgeable with the rules of trial procedure and rules of evidence you will face many objections by opposing counsel and you will become overwhelmed at the trial and your chances of success will be greatly diminished. Trial preparation can be an overwhelming process and it is very important to do your due diligence with respect to preparing your pleadings and your legal arguments and being able to address legal points that will come up during the trial. When you are preparing your various court papers, it can be helpful to review other court cases as court files are a matter of public record and you can learn a great deal from studying court pleadings in other cases that went to trial. For example, you can take jury instructions from another court case on a similar issue as your case and tailor those jury instructions for your case. You can do the same thing with other similar pleadings and tailor them to your case. Because most trials involve a multitude of documents, this in and of itself can be a potential problem for you to handle at the trial and will disrupt your thought process and the flow of the trial if you find yourself overwhelmed in keeping track of and looking for particular documents throughout the trial. For this reason, if you have somebody that is responsible and competent enough to help you keep track of the documents and help you stay organized at the trial, you can ask the judge for permission to allow this person to sit with you at the trial and assist you with the paperwork aspect of things. This would be a tremendous help to you and something that would be wise for you to consider.

Prospective Consultants to Justice for Pro Se's

Two excellent University of Chicago Law School students already mentioned, Phillip Acevedo and Brian Crush, have done yeoman work for me on the structure of my company, specifically its conversion to a 301(c)(3) nonprofit; effectively they have been, and I hope will remain until their graduation, consultants to my company. As additional consultants I hope to be able to "land" Kevin P. Durkin, a leading Chicago lawyer who is a past president of the Chicago Bar Association; Patrick Collins, another very prominent Chicago lawyer; Thomas Dart, the very distinguished Sheriff of Cook County, Illinois; Mark DeBofsky, head of a Chicago law firm that focuses on claims of pro se's for disability, health, life and retirement benefits; Father

David Link of Notre Dame, an expert (like company member Ken Abraham) on prison abuse of inmates; Claire DeMatteis, a distinguished prison reformer in Delaware; the very distinguished Chicago and New York consulting firm of Stout Rissius Ross, LLC (now called just Stout) and one of its very distinguished Chicago representatives, Dan Broadhurst, who heads up Stout's Dispute Resolution Group; Alison Siegler, the head of the criminal justice clinic at the University of Chicago Law School; and Professor David Zarfes—Associate Dean, Clinical Professor of Law, and Director, Kirkland & Ellis Corporate Clinic, all roles that he occupies as a member of the faculty of the University of Chicago Law School.

Here are the email addresses of, and some further information about, some of the prospective consultants:

Philip Acevedo, pacevedo@uchicago.edu;
Dan Broadhurst, Stout Rissius Ross, LLC, https://www.stoutadvisory.com/;
Patrick M. Collins, King & Spalding, https://www.kslaw.com/;
Brian Crush, bcrush@uchicago.edu;
Thomas J. Dart, https://en.wikipedia.org/wiki/Tom_Dart;
Mark DeBofsky, https://www.debofsky.com/About-Us/Mark-Debofsky.shtml;
Claire DeMatteis, https://whyy.org/articles/special-assistant-named-to-change-culture-in-delaware-prisons/;
Kevin P. Durkin, kpd@cliffordlaw.com, former President of the Chicago Bar Association;
Patrick Fitzgerald, https://www.skadden.com, who served for more than a decade as the U.S. Attorney for the Northern District of Illinois, and is now in practice at the Skadden firm in Chicago;
Father David T. Link, Dean Emeritus and Professor Emeritus at Notre Dame Law School, law.nd.edu/directory/david-link/;

Alison Siegler, head of the Federal Criminal Justice Clinic at University of Chicago Law School, https://www.law.uchicago.edu/faculty/siegler;

David Zarfes, https://www.wikilawschool.net/wiki/, Associate Dean, Clinical Professor of Law, and Director, Kirkland & Ellis Corporate Clinic, all at the University of Chicago Law School.

I have sent a note to each of the above inviting him or her to become a consultant to my company, and with the note this book to help them orient themselves to the needs and opportunities that the company presents. If as I hope all accept my invitation, that will bring to 13 the number of my consultants and thereby increase the number of members of my company from 71 to 84. I expect the total number eventually to soar above 100 as the company spreads into more and more states and into other U.S. territory as well.

Consultants will be free to use the company's suite of offices and meeting rooms on the fiftieth floor of 227 West Monroe Street in downtown Chicago.

Directors and Donors

Needing to create a board of directors, I have had the good fortune to be able to recruit eleven outstandingly able and experienced persons in business, law, the Illinois state legislature, and the academy to be members of the board:

Daniel Broadhurst, head of the Consulting Group at Stout, Rithius, Ross. https://www.stoutadvisory.com/professionals/daniel-broadhurst.

Lisa Colpoys, executive director of Illinois Legal AidOnline. https://www.https://www.linkedin.com/in/lcolpoys.

John J. Cullerton, President of the Illinois Senate. www.senatorcullerton.com.

Mark D. DeBofsky, head of well-known pro bono law firm in Chicago. https://www.debofsky.com.

George T. Dowd III, highly experienced business financier. www.globaleconomicsgroup.com/cv/GDowd_Resume%20(3).pdf.

Judge Joan B. Gottschall of the federal district court in Chicago. https://en.wikipedia.org/wiki/Joan_B._Gottschall.

Ashley Keller, a managing director at BurfordCapital. www.burfordcapital.com/directory/ashley-keller/.

Thomas J. Miles, dean of the University of Chicago Law School. https://www.law.uchicago.edu/faculty/miles.

Dennis Rendleman, ethics official of the American Bar Association. Dennis.Rendleman@americanbar.org.

Andrew Rosenfield, managing partner of Guggenheim Partners and also an official of The TTG Group. andrewrosenfield@gmail.com.

Selvyn Seidel, founder and chairman of Fulbrook Capital Management LLC. https://www.linkedin.com/in/selvyn-seidel-78a5979.

Ann Claire Williams, recently retired Seventh Circuit Federal Court of Appeals judge. www.chicagotribune.com/news/sns-bc-il--judge-retires-20171127-story.html.

The board will meet in the aforementioned suite of offices and meeting rooms. There will however be no evening meetings of the board, and video conferencing equipment will be installed in the office suite so that any director who for whatever reason can't or doesn't want to attend a meeting in person will be able to participate fully in the board meeting nevertheless. The directors will be compensated for their attendance, whether in person or by video, at the meetings, and my company will ensure that they are protected from litigation involving their membership and resulting involvement in Justice for Pro Se's. The standard form of protection for directors against liability is what is called D&O Insurance Coverage, of which there are three types. The first type, called Insuring Agreement A coverage (A-Side coverage), covers the right of directors (and also company officers) to receive direct payment from the insurer for defense costs and liability if they are sued, if they do not have a right to be indemnified, or if indemnification is not available because of insolvency. The second type of coverage is Insuring Agreement B coverage (B-Side coverage), which covers indemnification claims that directors and officers may make against the institution or entity under corporate law or the organizing documents of the institution or entity. The third type, Insuring Agreement C coverage (C-Side coverage), often referred to as entity coverage, insures the entity for its own wrongful acts, typically to cover securities claims and avoid an allocation of benefits between the company and the officers and directors. Insurers may provide one or more of the above types of coverage. In sum, a nonprofit—which Justice for Pro Se's is—should ensure D&O protection through any of the following types of insurance (A-Side, B-Side, or C-Side coverage). D&O Insurance protects employees and officers as well as directors, and typically provides unlimited coverage.

Here is additional information about each of the eleven confirmed directors:

Andrew Rosenfield is an economist and a lawyer. In 1977, he co-founded Lexecon, Inc. with Judge Richard Posner and Professor William Landes. He was its President and Chairman

for over twenty years. He is now a managing partner at Guggenheim Partners, LLC and a managing partner at The Greatest Good, an economics and philanthropic consulting firm. He is also a lecturer at the University of Chicago Law School. He has personally made available office space for Justice for Pro Se's at the Franklin Center at 227 W. Monroe St. in Chicago.

Ashley Keller is a lawyer and senior advisor at Burford Capital, though he is leaving Burford to start his own law firm. He co-founded Gerchen Keller Capital, which was acquired by Burford. He worked at Bartlit Beck Herman Palenchar and Scott LLP, a litigation boutique, and he was  also an analyst at Alyeska Investment Group. He clerked for Judge Richard Posner and for Justice Anthony Kennedy. He is also a lecturer at the University of Chicago Law School.

Daniel Broadhurst is the head of the Dispute Consulting group at Stout Risius Ross, LLC. Previously, he founded Natoma Partners, a financial consulting company. He also led the Disputes and Investigations practice at Huron Consulting Group.

Dennis Rendleman is the Chief Counsel for the American Bar Association's Standing Committee on Ethics and Professional Responsibility. He wrote *The Annotated Model Code of Judicial Conduct*. He taught legal studies at the University of Illinois at Springfield. He was General Counsel of the Illinois State Bar Association. He helped to draft the Illinois Rules of Professional Conduct based on the ABA Model Rules of Professional Conduct.

George Dowd led Foreign Exchange Sales for the Americas at Societe Generale. He previously worked at the foreign exchange desks of JP Morgan Chase and Bank of America. He also worked in trading and trading system development at Credit Suisse and Gelber Management, Inc.

Judge Joan Gotschall is a senior judge of the United States District Court for the Northern District of Illinois. She was nominated by President Bill Clinton in 1996 to the court and she took senior status in 2012. Prior to this appointment, she was a United States Magistrate for the Northern District of Illinois. She also previously worked as a staff attorney for the Federal Defender Program in Chicago and in private practice.

Mark DeBofsky is an employment litigation lawyer at DeBofsky, Sherman & Casciari, PC, and a professor at John Marshall Law School. He writes for the Chicago Daily Law Bulletin. He was a senior editor of Bloomberg's Employee Benefits Law.

Richard Posner is a retired judge of the Seventh Circuit Court of Appeals. He is the founder and executive director of Justice for Pro Se's. He is a lecturer at the University of Chicago. He previously founded Compass Lexecon with Andrew Rosenfield and William Landes. He is the author of 64 books.

Selvyn Seidel is the chairman of the Justice for Pro Se's Board of Directors. He is the founder and chairman of Fulbrook Capital Management, LLC. Before his current position, he founded and chaired Burford Capital. He was a litigation attorney for over forty years and he co-founded the New York office of Latham and Watkins. He has also taught at the New York University School of Law and at Oxford University.

I have chosen Selvyn Seidel to be the first chairman of the board of directors of my company. He is an outstanding businessman, notably generous, and with a deep interest in social matters and a strong commitment to helping pro se's. In addition Selvyn Seidel is generously playing a critical role in the formation of my board of directors. The reaction to my letter invitations to prospective directors was weak. Selvyn has voluntarily stepped into the gap, and is actively recruiting prospective directors both from within and without the group that I wrote to. I am immensely grateful to him. On March 16, the board, which had not yet met, had a conference call, though unfortunately because of technical problems only Mr. Seidel, Judge Gottschall, and I were audible.

Let me also say more about Dan Broadhurst, as dispute consulting is not likely to be a term with which most readers of this book are familiar. Dispute-resolution firms or components of firms are useful outlets for many purposes, including services in litigation, mediation, and arbitration. Stout is a major consulting firm in Chicago and New York, and its Chicago headquarters contains a dispute resolution branch headed by Dan Broadhurst, whom I have recruited to be a director of my company.

Dispute resolution can significantly reduce the costs and burdens of litigation and result in solutions not available in court. Mr. Broadhurst's experience ranges across complex litigation matters relating to international and domestic tax law, regulatory issues, breach of contract, intellectual property, fraud, tort, environmental, and claims against government agencies. His dispute-resolution efforts seek, for example, to make sure that a company client in a dispute has satisfied its fiduciary duties and is in compliance with regulations. He and his dispute-resolution team give expert testimony in regulatory proceedings, company disputes, or internal investigations, especially in tax or bankruptcy court. Recent examples include assisting an acquiring firm's board of directors to form an independent opinion for determining whether the transaction price was fair. Stout reviewed the transaction offer but also made site visits, conducted interviews with senior management of both the target and buyer, evaluated financial and operational risks, and assessed broader industry and market considerations. And upon completion of the merger transaction Stout was called on to help determine the allocation of the purchase price allocation for tax and financial reporting purposes. Stout is typically engaged by outside counsel to provide expert witnesses in cases such as a recent breach of contract action brought against a client that had terminated the plaintiff as a supplier. Stout also recently provided an expert witness in a case that involved breach of a franchise agreement.

Moving On Once Again

I am hopeful that within the limits of their responsibilities the directors will be generous donors to the company. But directors are not the only potential donors. Because the company will be a 501(c)(3) charitable foundation rather than a profit-making entity, it will be exempt from federal taxes, and donors to it will be exempt from having to pay federal income tax on their donations to the company. The importance of donations to a company such as mine deserves emphasis. Most legal services are financed by the fees that lawyers' clients pay their lawyers. That mode of financing is not open to me, because my clients are pro se's, and pro se's are by definition unable or unwilling to pay for legal services. Yet their lawyers or their nonlawyer legal advisors must be compensated, and an essential source of their compensation is donations.

Screening

I need to say something about the screening of applicants for assistance by my company. I receive, mainly from pro se's (including prison inmates, who constitute about half of all pro se's), a large number of emails, letters, packages of documents, and phone calls, all asking for help; and I have to decide whether there is enough possible merit in a communication to warrant my either responding to the communicant or referring the matter to a member of my company. The screening and forwarding process is difficult and time consuming, and I need help. I expect in a couple of months to be able to obtain much of the necessary help from company members, primarily Brian Vukadinovich but also Patrick Thesing, Bradley Fuller, Ken Abraham, Shon Hopwood, Sakina Carbide, Alan Popkin, and others. So far I have been doing most of the screening of the pro se's myself, and I can assure all members of the company that it's exhausting and to a degree unrewarding, though necessary, work, so it really has to be divided among company members. The principal problem I've encountered is verbosity. Pro se's are by definition not lawyers; often they are not well educated; a substantial fraction are prison inmates. Unsurprisingly a great many pro se's find it very difficult to present a lucid, cogent, readable summary of their case. Often the documents they submit to me or refer to lack a rational relation to their case. We need to deal with pro se's patiently; we need to be alert to the fact that many of them don't require, and are not best served by, being represented by a lawyer in court. They may need some out-of-court assistance by a lawyer, such the drafting of a complaint or a brief—what goes by the name of "ghostwriting," and is increasingly permitted by courts, as explained in a number of articles by Dennis Rendleman, a leading expert on legal ethics and now a member of my company. Also or instead the pro se may need instruction by a lawyer or other legal expert (such as company member Brian Vukadinovich, discussed at length earlier) in how to be one's own courtroom lawyer. And we need, as noted earlier, an exact tabulation of the number of pro se's whom we are assisting.

But I don't want to create the impression that mine is the only company in the domain of pro se litigation that recognizes the importance of training pro se's to be their own courtroom lawyers. Notably Courtroom5 (https://courtroom5.com/the-courts-are-ours/), mentioned earlier in this book, is a company in North Carolina that is both much like my company and, as noted below, much unlike my company. It is run by two women, Sonja Ebron (a member of my company) and Debra Slone. Neither is a lawyer. The firm's motto is *Be Your Own Lawyer.* As explained in a declaration by it entitled *About Us* (https:/courtroom5.com/about), the company's company—all nonlawyers like Ebron and Slone—teach pro se's how to handle their cases in court without a lawyer—how to be in effect their own lawyers.

Ms. Ebron has acknowledged the affinity between Courtroom5 and my company in her recent Courtroom5 comment that "A Good Year Is a Good Reason to Say Thank You" (https://courtroom5.com/category/pro-se-litigation/). She notes that "Judicial bias against pro se litigants is so common that it pays to expect and prepare for it. It's made a federal appeals court judge mad enough to quit the bench. Good for him! Judge Richard Posner is an ally."

Although as I said the firm has its headquarters in North Carolina, like my company it doesn't limit its activities to the state in which its headquarters are located. Indeed its ambitions like those of my company are nationwide, but the means of realizing those ambitions are different from those of my company. Her company does not represent pro se's in court; rather, it broadcasts, including in websites, advice to pro se's. By these means, and also by extensive circulation of spreadsheets containing large amounts of information about the work of the company, the company is able to reach an immense number of pro se's. But its interaction with individual pro se's is limited to cases in which a pro se responds to a communication on a website or broadcast from the company.

Having discussed our respective companies at length with Ms. Ebron I look forward to years of fruitful collaboration with her company—which I have to admit is at present in the lead in our partnership, for while I have representatives in 27 states and the District of Columbia committed to helping pro se's, Courtroom5 has provided service to pro se's in 38 states and the District of Columbia and is continuing to do so without abatement.

Highly pertinent to successful collaboration between our two companies is the fact that like Ms. Ebron and her partner Ms. Slone and their staff, many of our company members, most notably but not only Brian Vukadinovich, are not lawyers but use their intuitive legal knowledge and their experience in litigation to help pro se's learn to be their own courtroom lawyers. Remember that Mr. Vukadinovich, at the time a high school teacher and basketball coach in Indiana, was the pro se plaintiff in a suit against the high school, which had fired him—and won his suit (obtaining a $203,000 judgment) in federal district court despite the fact that the defendant was represented by five lawyers all of whom were in the courtroom every day of the trial. Ms. Slone and Ms. Ebron, and many of their team, resemble Mr. Vukadinovich in having trial experience as pro se's and now using that experience (which in the case of both Slone and Ebron is considerable, as explained in *About Us*) to train pro se's to be their own courtroom lawyers. (He is the author of the short, simple, but comprehensive "Pro Se Manual" (printed at pp. 36 to 44 above) used to train many pro se's to be their own courtroom lawyers.) It is essential that readers of this book understand that a lawyer is not a sine qua non for successful litigation by a person who has no lawyer—a pro se.

Mrs. Ebron happens to be not only thorough and energetic, but also colorful and vivid, as these questations from her show:

1. *On judges:* "What is it about wearing the black robe that leads judges to believe they can get away with these things? Are they simply worse than the rest of us? Are they corrupted by the power they hold? Is it the absence of real consequences when they're caught? I've come to believe it's a complete lack of accountability. We have the right to appeal crazy rulings, for sure. But that right is often as ephemeral as the right to represent oneself in court."

2. *On the limits of using lawyers:* "What does a lawyer do to contain his emotions surrounding the personal issues in the

case? Nothing, because they belong to his client. What can a lawyer tell a pro se litigant about handling the bias and trickery that opposing lawyers, court staff and judges deploy against non-lawyers? Not too much. Since non-lawyers are freed from the Rules of Professional Conduct, how can a lawyer—who is bound by those Rules—prepare a pro se litigant to operate outside them? Hard to imagine. No, lawyers can tell us how they win in court, but they play on a different field with different rules and equipment. We are forced to play a different game than they play."

3. *On judges dismissing pro se's:* "Even when pro se litigants come prepared for court, judges often patronize us (at best) or ignore us (at worst). We are tolerated long enough for the barest appearance of due process, then tossed aside by opposing counsel and a complicit judge who act like old college roommates."

4. *On the irrationality of the judicial system:* "It does us well to remember, when facing injustice, that process is all we can expect from our courts. Don't go looking for justice. Don't go looking for rational decisions, free of contradiction."

5. *On the importance of having a court reporter:* "That machine produces the only official record of what transpired at a hearing. Somehow the presence of that little typewriter transforms a raving lunatic on the bench into someone who actually wants to make a ruling that can stand up on appeal."

My one unsatisfied curiosity about Courtroom5 is how Ebron and Slone finance it, since pro se's do not pay lawyers' fees unless they hire lawyers just as "ghostwriters"—who as I explained earlier are lawyers who write a brief or other document that a pro se can brandish in court without having to acknowledge that he is not the author—indeed, pro se's who hire lawyers to represent them in court thereby cease to be pro se's. I am guessing that the source of the company's money is not as one might expect donations but is instead the damages that the two women obtain in suits they bring pro se. As Courtroom5's website makes clear, the women are very active litigants—and also very successful ones.

I have spoken at length recently with Ms. Ebron. She looks forward as do I to collaboration between our two companies, bearing in mind that like her and her partner Ms. Slone and their staff many of our company members, most notably but not only the aforementioned Brian Vukadinovich, are not lawyers but use their intuitive legal knowledge and experience to help pro se's learn to be their own courtroom lawyers. Remember that Mr. Vukadinovich was the pro se plaintiff in a suit against the public school system that had fired him—and won his suit (obtaining a $203,000 judgment) despite the fact that the defendant was represented by five lawyers all of whom were in the courtroom every day of the trial. Miss Slone and Miss Ebron, and many of their team, resemble Mr. Vukadinovich in having trial experience as pro se's and now using that experience (which in the case of both Slone and Ebron is considerable, as explained in *About Us*) to train pro se's to be their own courtroom lawyers. I look forward to a long and successful collaboration between my company and Courtroom5.

Ms. Ebron has been kind enough to furnish me and Mr. Vukadinovich with an elaborate set of spreadsheets for recording information about the pro se's who seek the help of my company, and also about the assistance given to the pro se's by members of the company. Here is a spreadsheet for my company modeled on Ms. Ebron's spreadsheets.

Client Name	Volunteer	State	Claim Type	Client Role	Representation	Start Date	Status
Pro Se Client 1	A	OH	Business	Defendant	Pro Se	03/01/18	Completed
Pro Se Client 2	B	MI	Business	Defendant	Pro Se	03/02/18	Active
Pro Se Client 3	C	KY	Prisoner	Petitioner	Pro Bono	03/02/18	Active
Pro Se Client 4	D	WV	Foreclosure	Defendant	Pro Bono	03/05/18	Active
Pro Se Client 5	C	OH	Family	Respondent	Pro Se	03/05/18	Initiated

Volunteer Statistics				
Volunteer	Initiated	Active	Completed	Total
Volunteer A	0	0	0	0
Volunteer B	0	0	0	0
Volunteer C	0	0	0	0
	0	0	0	0
	0	0	0	0

and himself a former prison inmate, is a fre[...]
a formidable critic of American prison co[...]
frequently ghastly, and which my company [...]
must continue to endeavor to seek improv[...]

Also getting increased attention is the [...]
police abuse of custody, as when police [...]
(sometimes fatally) beat up or even shoot [...]
arrest. Our company member Brian Vukad[...]
me recently his own experience with poli[...]
Here is his report, slightly edited by me: "I [...]
of police perjury evidence that surfaced [...]
false arrests against me that it is mind bog[...]
well how significant of a problem of epide[...]
this is. This is an area that I believe my c[...]
lot of good things with. Laquan McDonald [...]
to death by Chicago police) is a classic exa[...]
will abuse people and then lie about it an[...]
get away with it. Fortunately, people who h[...]
able to record videos of McDonald's mu[...]
officers are currently in trouble for going a[...]
officer who pulled the trigger—by lying on [...]
that McDonald was going toward them w[...]
going away from them. Because the case b[...]
public issue (having been recorded by vic[...]
no problem obtaining representation. But m[...]
help that I [this is still Brian Vukadinovich s[...]
from people unable to afford legal represen[...]
of representing themselves. I have no dou[...]
unfortunately many people are being abu[...]
custody. Justice for Pro Se's could be a gre[...]
ing with the problem, I believe."

Ken Abraham happens also to be an excellent chronicler of police custody abuse. See the following articles by him (a brief selection of his copious output): "Baltimore Police Officer Accidentally Records Himself Planting Drugs At Crime Scene" (http://www.citizensforcriminaljustice.net/baltimore-police-officer-accidentally-records-planting-drugs-crime-scene-prosecute-ass-kra/); "Chicago Police Had A Secret Black Site Where They Treated Petty-Criminals Like Terrorists" (http://www.citizensforcriminaljustice.net/chicago-police-secret-black-site-treated-petty-criminals-like-terrorists-amazing-kra/); "Police Let K-9 [i.e., a dog] Maul Handcuffed Unconscious Man's Face as They Beat Him to Death" (http://www.citizensforcriminaljustice.net/police-let-k-9-maul-handcuffed-unconscious-mans-face-beat-death); "Georgia Cop Sentenced to Life in Prison for Tasering Handcuffed Man to Death. The only reason this is sure to send shock waves throughout the law enforcement community is that too few are held accountable" (http://www.citizensforcriminaljustice.net/georgia-cop-sentenced-life-prison-tasering-handcuffed-man-death/).

These are just four of the more than 30 articles on abuses of custody by police that Abraham has written or published recently. But for completeness I have to note a recent article by Clive Stafford Smith, "Judge dread: Why the U.S. justice system is not fit for purpose" (*Times Literary Supplement*, December 1, 2017, p. 30)—a devastating indictment of U.S. criminal law. I also want to mention a splendid piece of writing by Jesse Hogin, a member of Theresa Yuan's research team at the University of Chicago Law School who is soon to join Justice for Pro Se's. In a nine-page analysis of public defenders (government lawyers who represent pro se's in court), dated February 6, 2018, available on request from Hogin or Theresa Yuan or me, and entitled "Recent Suits About the Ineffective Assistance of [that is, provided by] Public Defenders," Hogin makes a compelling presentation of the shocking deficiencies in public defender programs.

I'll end this section by reporting on a very recent, and as it seems to me a very disagreeable, decision in a police custody case—more precisely a multi-lawyer discussion on the internet of a decision that is not named. The fullest discussion reveals that the decedent (who was highly intoxicated and alone in his residence) called 911 and said they should send an ambulance to his house because he was going to commit suicide. The officers responding to the call knew he was alone because of prior interactions with him that evening. When they arrived at his house, they called out to him and he told them to leave him alone and go away. They opened the door to the house and crossed the threshold, at which point they encountered him holding a gun to his head. They told him to put the gun down, and when he took the gun away from his head, one officer Tasered him and the other shot and killed him. The body camera video does not show what he did with the gun when he took it away from his head (the camera's view was blocked by a door frame) but the shooter claims the gun was pointed at him. The officer who fired the Taser says he didn't see where it was pointed, just that it wasn't pointed at the decedent's head any longer. The officers' initial conduct of entering the home when there was no danger to anyone else was probably unjustified. After that, their conduct may have become more justified because they encountered the decedent holding a gun. Is anyone familiar with similar scenarios, and whether the initial violation of the 4th Amendment renders the subsequent conduct improper, even though the subsequent conduct might not have been improper on its own?

I added my two cents to the internet discussion, saying "I don't agree that 'the officers' initial conduct of entering the home when there was no danger to anyone else was probably unjustified.' They obviously thought and were justified in thinking that there was a suicide risk, and there is nothing wrong with trying to prevent a person from committing suicide. The only issue I think is whether shooting the person was justified; for surely the entry into the home was. It's impossible to say whether it was justified, because we don't know whether the resident was pointing his gun at either of the officers when he was fatally shot."

And a Brief Note on Legal Ethics

My earlier mention of Dennis Rendleman brings to mind a brush I had early in the life of my company with issues of legal ethics, when I received messages from some members suggesting that the company was violating or in danger of violating rules of legal ethics. The most sustained messaging of this character came from Michael E. McCabe, Jr., of the McCabe Ethics Law firm, who later quit my company because I didn't buy his criticisms of the company's ethics.

I didn't understand most of his complaints. They struck me as trivial and fussy, though I agreed with him that if a member of a firm represents a client, another member of the firm cannot (while remaining a member) represent the client's adversary. For that would place the firm on both sides of the case! Beyond that I did not and do not see the point or merit of McCabe's ethical accusations. In 35 and 2/3 years as a federal appellate judge, I was accused of an ethical violation exactly once—by Chief Judge Diane Wood of the Seventh Circuit Court of Appeals, last summer. She falsely accused me of violating the federal judicial Codes of Conduct, the falsity lying in her failure to understand that the Codes are purely advisory, not mandatory, and specifically that the particular provision that she accused me of violating—Opinion No. 55. which concerns extrajudicial publication by federal judges—begs—not orders—judges to be cautious about publication that might invite unmerited criticism of the judiciary. Incidentally, although I have been a lawyer since I graduated from Harvard Law School in 1962—55 years ago—Judge Wood's accusation was the only accusation of unethical conduct by me in that entire period.

I need to know more about legal ethics than I do, and to that end I have embarked on a book-length project on the subject, with the aid of my research team at the University of Chicago Law School. Yet I see at present no rational objection, ethical or otherwise, to the structure I've created for my company with the indispensable aid of colleagues such as Ken Abraham and Brian Vukadinovich. The firm consists primarily of lawyers but includes nonlawyers, who are not permitted to hold themselves out as lawyers or to appear in court representing clients, thereby acting as lawyers, but are permitted to advise people—these will mainly be pro se's—on how to handle themselves in court. And with the relaxation of the ban against "ghostwriting," a pro se will in a growing number of states (such as Illinois) now be allowed to hire a lawyer who will not appear in court but who will have written a brief or other document for the pro se without his assistance being acknowledged in the courtroom.

A number of lawyers who have joined my firm are already members of law firms in the states in which they practice. They may have to get their firms' consent to take on cases that the firm itself has not agreed to take on. Fine; as long as the analysis I've been describing is adhered to, I see no ethical problems. Obviously any member of the firm who disagrees is free to resign. The fact that Dennis Rendleman is now a member makes such resignations unlikely. He is a formidable figure in the world of legal ethics: he is ethics counsel in the American Bar Association's Center for Professional Responsibility and also counsel to the ABA Standing Committee on Ethics and Professional Responsibility. I expect him to play a major role in my company, and not merely as a member of the board of directors. Here is some pertinent information about him: He is admitted to the practice of law in Illinois state courts, in the Seventh Circuit federal court, and in the U.S. Supreme Court. His preferred email address is darendleman@sbcglobal.net but he can also be contacted at 217-725-6443 (his personal cell) or his ABA office 312-988-0518, but he prefers not to be contacted directly by potential clients by cold calls. Also he is not in a position to handle individual direct representation, but he has volunteered to provide advice to lawyers and nonlawyers in my firm who have ethical issues.

As Ethics Counsel at the ABA, Mr. Rendleman works on ABA Model Rules of Professional Conduct and ABA Model Code of Judicial Conduct, amendments thereto, and opinions interpreting them as approved by the ABA Standing Committee on Ethics and Professional Responsibility. He is also able to research issues arising in individual states or specific jurisdictions regarding ethics, admission and discipline, and he has experience authoring and editing appellate briefs and memos, though his present time constraints limit him to editing and consulting rather than researching and authoring; but he may also be able to assist in reviewing some intake or screening of written communications received.

I want to close this brief discussion of ethics by quoting three messages I received from members of my firm (pre-Rendleman) concerning ethical issues, one from Ken Abraham and the other two (the first long, the second short) from Brian Vukadinovich:

Ken:

"Hi Dick,

As you know, I have a fairly low opinion of Bar Associations insofar as their control (and lack thereof!) of lawyers is concerned, but, of course, every member of Justice for Pro Se's should take pains to act ethically at all times.

I do think that whatever case management system (computer software thingee) we use should have a check for conflicts of interest, so that one member cannot undertake a case against the interests of a client being helped by another member. I would think that is a "given".

Well, that's my unsolicited two cents.

Good night.

Ken"

Brian 1:

"Hi Dick,

I read the recently raised issues and as a "non-lawyer" I don't want to jump in out of place so I am not going to send this out as a mass email to everybody. It is good that the range of people are expressing their viewpoints on potential "conflict of interest" issues, etc., but there may perhaps be a bit of "over-lawyering" going on to a certain extent. For example, Mr. Michael McCabe cited 'issues regarding non-lawyers being held out as "members" of the PLG [Posner Law Group, an earlier name of my company], and regarding de-facto partnering of lawyers with non-lawyers when any part of the business of the Group involves the practice of law.' But there is no rule or law that forbids a "non-lawyer" from assisting a lawyer in a case. Firms all over the country utilize "non-lawyers" to a great extent in various litigations. A simple random googling of law firms usually will end up showing the law firm listing names and in many cases even pictures of the "non-lawyers" on the law firms' websites. The "non-lawyers" in many cases are secretaries, paralegals, etc., but also may be investigators or experts who are experts in assisting lawyers. Why expect this to be different for your firm? As for the "conflict of interest" issue raised by Mr. McCabe wherein he questioned what would happen if a pro se was being assisted by a member of the firm and another member was asked for assistance on the opposing end of the case; it's very simple, it should be treated the same way as it would be treated by any other law firm: another member of the same firm mustn't agree to handle the adversary's part of the case. If this ever happened, then as soon as it became known that another member of the firm was assisting a pro se party in a particular matter, the member asked to assist the opposing party would decline assistance, to avoid a conflict of interest. The opinion by the American Bar Association Standing Committee on Ethics and Professional Responsibility "Undisclosed Legal Assistance to Pro Se Litigants" (May 5, 2007) puts to rest almost all of the concerns, but I just thought I would throw in my thoughts. Feel free to consider them or toss them aside if you would like."

Brian 2:

"Hi Dick,

"I just read your communication to McCabe that McCabe attached for everybody to read. You did a great job in letting him know that the generalities he threw out were nothing more than generalities and that he needs to be more specific. I agree with you 100% that he threw around too many generalities and should have backed them up with specifics rather than opening up a chaotic can of worms that for the most part was unnecessary and unhelpful. There didn't seem to be much common sense in what he was saying and he certainly didn't back up anything he said either at the time he said what he said and certainly not afterward when you asked him to do so. Good job!"

Moving On

Doubtless many readers of this book are familiar with the first and second editions of my recent book, mainly though not entirely concerned with the plight of pro se's. The first edition—*Reforming the Federal Judiciary: My Former Court Needs to Overhaul Its Staff Attorney Program and Begin Televising Its Oral Arguments*—was published on September 7, 2017, and was 301 pages in length; the much longer second edition (433 pages)—*Improving the Federal Judiciary: Staff Attorney Programs, the Plight of the Pro Se's, and the Televising of Oral Arguments*—was published on December 4, 2017, and as it places even greater emphasis than the first edition does on the plight of pro se's, I particularly recommend it.

But here I just want to distinguish between prisoner pro se's and other pro se's, because I've learned more about the differences between the two groups than I knew when I wrote the two books. The non-prisoner pro se's are generally in search of financial compensation for alleged infringement of their legal rights, while the prisoner pro se's generally focus on obtaining early release from prison. The aims of the non-prisoner pro se's are similar to those of other civil litigants, and with proper assistance from lawyers or others they are in a good position to obtain the relief sought, at least in part. The situation of the prisoners is very different. Mainly they want to be released from prison before—very often long, long before—the expiration of their sentences. The desire is often quite reasonable because prison sentences in the United States tend to be excessively long. But the obstacle to the relief sought by prisoners, rarely overcome, is that the normal time for challenging a sentence as too long is during the sentencing hearing that follows the criminal trial. There are exceptions: the prisoner may have been subjected to severe brutality during his incarceration; a critical error in the sentence imposed may be discovered long after the defendant has been languishing in prison; illness or age may have made the prisoner unfit to remain incarcerated. But these grounds for early discharge rarely succeed. Prisoners repeatedly seek habeas corpus in federal courts, not realizing that federal habeas corpus is almost impossible to obtain and often failing to invoke a more obtainable ground of relief.

What makes the pro se prisoner's plight especially distressing is the frequency of brutal treatment of prison inmates, often by guards rather than by other inmates, and often taking the form of totally inadequate medical care; I gave examples in the second edition of my previous book as well as earlier in this book. A recent article brought to my attention by Ken Abraham underscores the serious problem of violence in American prisons both by inmates against each other and staff, and by staff against inmates: Ames Alexander and Gavin Off, "Video captures inmate brutally attacking her [a member of the prison staff] for 43 seconds. Why didn't anyone help?" *Charlotte Observer*, Oct. 28, 2017—a long article but very worth reading.

Three Lists

In still another shift of focus, I now explain three critical lists of personnel involved in, sought by, or otherwise pertinent to my company:

List 1. All members of my company should already have received a list of all members, alphabetized by the first letter of each member's first name. The list will have to be revised from time to time as the membership alters; when that happens a new list will be sent. But here is the current list, with the listed lawyers italicized (remember that not all members of the company are lawyers), their email addresses given, and the states in which they are headquartered noted. The reader will notice that this list is a somewhat pruned version of the previously mailed one, because the previous one had included several persons whom I had not consulted about joining the company and who on reflection struck me as unlikely to join, and so I have deleted them. Here is the current list:

Amanda Vanderhorst, www.katesbarlow.com
Andrew Rosenfield, Illinois, andrewrosenfield@gmail.com
Aaron Van Oort, Minnesota, Aaron.VanOort@faegrebd.com
Abbe Gluck, Connecticut, abbe.gluck@yale.edu
Aknur Shah, Illinois, ashah@shahlegalrep.com

Alan S. Frankel, Illinois, alan.frankel@coherentecon.com
Alan Popkin, Missouri, alan.popkin@outlook.com
Alison Siegler, Illinois, alisonsiegler@uchicago.edu
Bradley Fuller, bafuller82@gmail.com
Brandon Sample, Vermont, Brandon@brandonsample.com
Brian Vukadinovich, Indiana, bvukadinovich@hotmail.com
Charito Calvachil-Mateyko, Delaware, charitocw@aol.com
Charles Blackman, Rhode Island, cblackman@levyblackman.com
Charles Silvestri Higgins, Tennessee, chiggins@bpjlaw.com
Christopher Ogolla. Texas, cogolla@savannahlawschool.org
Dan Johnson, Illinois, Dan@progressivepublicaffairs.com
Daniel Klerman, California, dklerman@law.usc.edu
David Lat, New York, davidbenjaminlat@gmail.com
David McCarthy, Illinois, dmccarthy@schiffhardin.com
Deborah Davis, South Carolina, d.davis@dicksondavislaw.com
Dennis Rendleman, Illinois, Dennis.Rendleman@americanbar.org
Devon M. Jacob, Pennsylvania, jacob@jacoblitigation.com
Dick Posner, Illinois, rposner62@gmail.com
Edward Blum, Maine, EBlum@aei.org
Eli Jacobs, New York, ejacobs@essexmgm.com
Eric J. Segall, Georgia, esegall@gsu.edu
Eric Posner, Illinois, eric_posner@law.uchicago.edu
Gary Peeples, Kentucky, gpeeples@bpjlaw.com
George T. Dowd III, Illinois, george@georgedowd.com
George W. Rumsey, Illinois, gwrumsey@att.net
Gordon Smith, Florida, gordonsmith67@hotmail.com
Gregory Sidak, D.C., jgsidak@criterionecono
James Dawson, Illinois, dawson.james@aol.com
James Geiser, Maryland, jhgeiser@umich.edu
James V. Cook, Florida, cookjv@gmail.com
Janet Carter, New York, janet.carter@gmail.com
John L. Kane, Colorado, john_l_kane@cod.uscourts.gov

Jonathan R. Zell, Ohio, JonathanZell@caa.columbia.edu
Justin Schwartz, Illinois, justinschwartzlaw@gmail.com
Ken Abraham, Delaware, kenabraham3138@gmail.com
Larry Downes, California, larry@larrydownes.com
Lawrence Lessig, Boston, lessig@law.harvard.edu
Matthew Dowd, mjdowd@dowdpllc.com
Matthew Freda, Tennessee, https://www.immigrantcivilrights.com/
Pamela McKinney, Illinois, pameladmckinney@gmail.com
Patrick Thesing, Texas, gadbois2015@gmail.com
R. Andrew Free, Tennessee, Andrew@immigrantcivilrights.com
Rachel Sachs. Missouri, rachel e. sachs@gmail.com
Rebecca Stone, California, rebeccastone1000@gmail.com
Richard W. Porter, Illinois, rporter@kirkland.com
Robert Sanford, Nebraska, bobandsuesanford@comcast.net
Robert S. Bruer, rob@bruerlaw.com
Ryan T. Holt, Tennessee, rholt@srvhlaw.com
Sakina Carbide, Illinois, carbidelaw@gmail.com
Selvyn Seidel, New York, sseidel@fulbrookmanagement.com
Shana Pollak, Nevada, lotsoflovebuddies@yahoo.com
Shon Hopwood, D.C., Shon.Hopwood@law.georgetown.edu
Sonja Ebron, Sonja@courtroom5.com
Starsha Sewell, Illinois, starshasewell@gmail.com
Stephen Abeyta, sjabeyta@gmail.com
Theresa Yuan, Illinois, theresayuan@uchicago.edu
Thomas Miles, Illinois, tmiles@law.uchicago.edu
Tom Gorman, California, tomgorman@gmail.com
William Landes, Illinois, w-landes@uchicago.edu

List 2. On October 20 I emailed all 88 of my former law clerks (except my four last law clerks, for they had left my employ when I retired from the Seventh Circuit Court of Appeals on September 2, 2017)) to tell them about the new firm and invite them to become members. Only two accepted the invitation. The firm was pretty rudimentary back in October, and so recently I re-sent the October 20 document to all its recipients in the hope that a nontrivial number would become members and therefore appear on list no. 1 as well. At this writing, only three have done so (and so they do appear on List 1 as well as on List 2). They are Daniel Klerman and Lawrence Lessig, prominent law professors at the University of California and Harvard University respectively, and Gregory Sidak, who heads an economics consulting firm (Criterion Economics, LLC) in Washington D.C. I hope to generate interest among others.

Here is the October 20 list. I am sure that recipients of this memorandum who are not on the list will recognize at least some of the names, and I am hopeful that many of the recipients, in addition to the three just mentioned, will now join the firm.

Aaron Van Oort	avanoort@faegre.com
Adam Hallowell	adam.hallowell@gmail.com
Andrew Baak	andrew.baak@bartlit-beck.com
Andrew Coan	andrew.coan@gmail.com
Andy Shapiro	andyshapiro@gmail.com
Ann Jaworski	annjaworski@gmail.com
Ashley Keller	ashckeller@gmail.com
Ashutosh Bhagwat	profbhagwat@gmail.com
Bill Ridgway	bill.ridgway@gmail.com
Bill Rinner	rinner@gmail.com
C. Scott Hemphill	hemphill@nyu.edu
Carolyn Shapiro	cshapiro1@kentlaw.edu
Charlie Wysong	cdwysong@gmail.com
Christopher Hampson	chris@hampson.us
Dan Siegfried	siegfried@uchicago.edu
Daniel Klerman	dklerman@law.usc.edu
David Greenwald	davidgreenwald@outlook.com
David Webb	dwebb@jd17.law.harvard.edu

Dennis Black	dennisdblackdc@gmail.com
Edward Dumont	edward.dumont@doj.ca.gov
Edward Morrison	emorri@law.columbia.edu
Erika Singer	erika.k.singer@gmail.com
Eugene Kontorovich	ekontorovich@gmail.com
Eva Saks	nyevita@aol.com
Gregory Barton	glb190@sbcglobal.net
Helaine Morrison	hmorrison@hallcapital.com
Herwig Schlunk	herwig.schlunk@vanderbilt.edu
Ileana Ciobanu	imciobanu@yahoo.com
Israel Friedman	israel.friedman@hotmail.com
J. Gregory Sidak	jgsidak@criterioneconomics.com
Jacob Goldin	jsgoldin@gmail.com
Janet Carter	janet.carter@gmail.com
Jay Richardson	richarjn@gmail.com
Jeffrey Chanin	jchanin@kvn.com
Jeffrey Cohen	jeffrey.cohen@linklaters.com
Jennifer Nou	jennifer.nou@gmail.com
Jim Talent	jtalent@bannerpublicaffairs.com
John Karin	johnisaackkarin@gmail.com
Jonathon Lewinsohn	Jlewinsohn@gmail.com
Jonathon Masur	jmasur@uchicago.edu
Julia Schwartz	julia.k.schwartz@gmail.com
Kate Shaw	kate.a.shaw@gmail.com
Katharine Silbaugh	silbaugh@bu.edu
Kathryn Judge	kjudge@gmail.com
Kevin Kordana	kk3t@virginia.edu
Kevin Ranlett	kevin.ranlett@gmail.com
Larry Downes	larry@larrydownes.com
Larry Lessig	lessig@law.harvard.edu
Lee Mason	leemason14@gmail.com
Lisa Heinzerling	lisaheinzerling@gmail.om
Maria Ponomarenko	maria.ponomarenko@gmail.com
Mark Savignac	mark.savignac@gmail.com
Mary Schnoor	mary.schnoor@gmail.com

Matthew Kugler	matthew.b.kugler@gmail.com
Matthew Rozen	matthewrozen@gmail.com
Matthew Spence	matthewjohnspence@gmail.com
Max Straus	mstraus@jd17.law.harvard.edu
Michael Green	msgre2@wm.edu
Michael Lindsay	lindsay.michael@dorsey.com
Miriam Hinman	miriam.hinman@gmail.com
Nat Love	natlove@gmail.com
Nathan Christensen	nchristensen@gmail.com
Peggy Barton	peggy.barton14@gmail.com
Rachel Sachs	rachel.e.sachs@gmail.com
Randal Picker	r-picker@uchicago.edu
Rebecca Haw	rebeccahaw@gmail.com
Rebecca Stone	rebeccastone1000@gmail.com
Richard Husseini	richard.husseini@bakerbotts.com
Richard Levy	rlevy@ku.edu
Richard Porter	rporter@kirkland.com
Robert Hochman	rhochman@sidley.com
Robert Loeb	rloeb@orrick.com
Robert Sitkoff	rsitkoff@law.harvard.edu
Ryan Hagglund	rhagglund@comcast.net
Sandra Glover	sandra.glover@usdoj.gov
Sean Driscoll	skdriscoll@gmail.com
Shawn Crincoli	scrincoli@tourolaw.edu
Shelley Murphey	smurphey@gmail.com
Sopan Joshi	sopan.joshi@alumni.stanford.edu
Steve Horowitz	sjhorowitz@gmail.com
Steve McAllister	stevemac@ku.edu
Tacy Flint	tacy.flint@gmail.com
Thane Rehn	thane.rehn@gmail.com
Timothy Shapiro	timothy.shapiro@gmail.com
Timothy Wu	wu@pobox.com
Tom Gorman	tomgorman@gmail.com
Ward (Pete) Farnsworth	wardfarnsworth@gmail.com
Yair Listokin	yair.listokin@yale.edu

List 3. My third list, embracing each state in which my firm does not yet have staff, lists the names of all the lawyers, law firms, or nonlawyer advisors whom I have contacted in the state by email or telephone to invite affiliation with my company. I tell them "You have worked on [insert type of case] pro bono in the past. Would you be interested in joining my panel of pro bono lawyers? I am hoping to assign to you meritorious cases in [name of state]. Should you be unable to take on a particular case, I am hoping that you could recommend one or two other good lawyers in your state who could take on the case."

This is not meant to be a full-time, paid position, and I will adjust case assignments based on your month-to-month workload. If you accept my invitation and join my company, you will have access to a nationwide panel of lawyers discussing judicial reform and swapping advice. I will be regularly seeking your suggestions regarding my company's development and strategies. I will also be available to discuss cases you've accepted from my company, which you can claim affiliation with on your firm's website and newsletters so that they can reach out directly to you. I am customizing each email based on the recipient's area of legal expertise.

Thus I aim to make my firm nationwide not by stationing members of the existing staff in these other states and other possessions, but rather by inviting a selection of active lawyers and legal advisors in all U.S. states and territories to associate with my firm not as employees of it but as affiliates willing to devote some time to providing advice and other services in their states or territories similar to the services that my firm provides in the states in which it has staff. We'll assist the affiliates in a variety of ways, including advice, loan of staff, and financial assistance, in that way making ours a truly nationwide firm serving a very large number of pro se's and others in need of legal advice and assistance. Every lawyer in list 3 is a lawyer whom I would like to be able to refer a pro se case to; many of these lawyers have, I know, a pro bono practice, which means they have represented pro se's, pro bono (that is, without charging them), in the past. Should a particular such lawyer be unable to take on a particular case, I am hoping he or she will recommend one or two other first-rate lawyers in the state who would be willing to take on the case. Membership in the list is not intended to connote a full-time, paid position, and I will therefore adjust case assignments in accordance with month-to-month workload.

Even in states in list 3 in which my firm is already represented by a lawyer or by a nonlawyer legal advisor, additional lawyers, advisors, etc. are named whom I or other members of my firm plan to contact in situations in which our representatives lack the time to accept new cases.

I have boldfaced the names of lawyers in this third list whom I deem to be of high priority because of exceptional aptitude or experience (for example in handling prisoner pro se cases). And for states in which my company already has representatives I indicate in list 3 that those representatives are already committed to my company.

The point that needs especially to be emphasized about all three lists and indeed about this entire book is the voluntary character of membership in or association with my firm. Not only is no one required to join the firm; no one is required to do anything once he or she has joined. Obviously I hope that members will provide assistance, whether in the form of representation or advice, to pro se's or others seeking and worthy of assistance. And the less they do, the less compensation they will receive from the firm. But the decision whether to assist or not, and if the former when and how often to assist, is entirely the decision of the member or affiliate in question, and not of me or anyone else. But they should bear in mind that as the firm's finances, which are dependent on donations, crystallize, which should be soon, I will be able to offer compensation for the assistance that members render to my firm's clients.

Enough about list 3 in the abstract—here it is in the concrete!

Alabama

1. **Nikaa Jordan at Lightfoot, Franklin, White, LLC**
    a. Jordan handles Alabama state appeals, and death sentence cases pro bono in the Alabama Court of Criminal Appeals.
    b. Phone: 205-581-0745
    c. Email: njordan@lightfootlaw.com
2. **A. Lane Morrison at Lightfoot, Franklin, White, LLC**
    a. Morrison handles mainly commercial cases, but has also worked pro bono on landlord-tenant disputes. He was recognized by the Birmingham Bar's Volunteer Lawyer's Program for his work in a landlord-tenant dispute.
    b. Phone: 205-581-0799
    c. Email: lmorrison@lightfoodlaw.com
3. Roger Bates at Hand, Arrendall, LLC
    a. Bates handles business litigation, healthcare disputes, and labor and employment cases.
    b. Phone: 205-324-4400
    c. Email: rbates@handarendall.com

Alaska

1. **Joshua Decker at the American Civil Liberties Union of Alaska**
    a. Decker, a University of Chicago law school graduate, is now the executive director of the American Civil Liberties Union's Alaska office. In the past he had worked on police-brutality cases in Chicago and helped rural, low-income individuals in Tennessee.
    b. Phone: 773-412-9368
    c. Email: decker.joshua@gmail.com
    d. Alternate email: acluak@acluak.org

Arizona

1. **Robert A. Mandel at Mandel Young, LLC**
   a. Mandels handles appeals in Arizona and he is licensed to practice at both the state and the federal level. He is a University of Michigan alum and is personally recommended by Jesse Hogin, a research assistant on Justice for Pro Se's currently at the University of Michigan.
   b. Phone: 602-374-2657
   c. Email: rob@mandelyoung.com
2. Kathy Brody at the American Civil Liberties Union of Arizona
   a. Brody worked on criminal defense cases before she became the legal director of the ACLU of Arizona.
   b. Phone: 602-650-1854
3. Matthew W. Bartz at Suzuki Law Offices
   a. Bartz works on criminal defense cases and he is licensed to practice law at both the state and federal level.
   b. Phone: 602-682-5270
   c. Email: matt@suzukilawoffices.com
4. David A. Black
   a. Black works on criminal defense cases and is licensed to practice law at the state level.
   b. Phone: 480-280-8028
   c. Email: david@dbphoenixcriminallawyer.com

Arkansas

1. Heidi Jamison at Legal Aid of Arkansas
   a. Jamison works on elderly assistance cases for the Legal Aid of Arkansas organization. She is licensed to practice at the state level.

       b. Phone: 479-442-0600 ext. 6301
       c. Email: hjamison@arlegalaid.org
2. Janet Dyer at Legal Aid of Arkansas
       a. Dyer works for the River Valley Volunteer Attorney Project. She is licensed to practice at the state level.
       b. Phone: 479-785-5211 ext. 4314
       c. Email: jdyer@arkansaslegalservices.org
3. Lora Crawley at the Center for Arkansas Legal Services
       a. Crawley works at the Center for Arkansas Legal Services. She is licensed to practice at the state level.
       b. Phone: 501-376-3423
       c. Email: lcrawley@arkansaslegalservices.org
4. Central Arkansas Legal Services
       a. This organization works on civil rights, bankruptcy, education, and employment cases. You can make contact with them to refer Arkansas cases to them.
       b. Phone: 501-376-3423
5. Tinsley and Youngdahl, PLLC
       a. This firm works on indigent defense and civil litigation.
       b. Phone: 501-683-8361

California

1. Katherine Macfarlane (Already committed to Justice for Pro Se's)
2. **Katherine Schon Brockway at Latham & Watkins in Menlo Park**
       a. Brockway works on intellectual property cases but she won an Impact Award for her pro bono work for a sex-trafficking survivor. She is

licensed to practice at the California state level, and also at the Illinois state level.
  b. Phone: 650-463-4668
  c. Email: Katherine.brockway@lw.com
3. **Brian Ahn at Latham & Watkins, LLC in Los Angeles**
   a. Ahn works on corporate securities law but he also works pro bono. He is a graduate of the University of Chicago Law School and in the past has worked on international human rights cases. He is licensed to practice at the state level.
   b. Phone: 213-891-9398
   c. Email: brian.ahn@lw.com
4. **Diana Aguilar at Latham & Watkins, LLC in San Francisco**
   a. Aguilar works on antitrust and competition cases but also maintains a pro bono practice for immigration and civil rights cases. She is licensed to practice at the state level.
   b. Phone: 415-395-8025
   c. Email: diana.aguilar@lw.com
5. David I. Adams at Latham & Watkins, LLC in San Francisco
   a. Adams works on commercial disputes, white collar defense cases, competition litigation, and intellectual property cases, but he also maintains a pro bono practice for immigration and asylum claims. He is licensed to practice at the state level.
   b. Phone: 415-646-7806
   c. Email: david.adams@lw.com
6. Thomas Alcorn at Latham & Watkins, LLC in Los Angeles
   a. Alcorn works on finance cases but also on pro bono on cases involving children and indigents. He is licensed to practice at the state level.
   b. Phone: 213-891-7358
   c. Email: Thomas.alcorn@lw.com

7. Winston Y. Chan at Gibson Dunn, LLC in San Francisco
    a. Chan works on white collar criminal defense, securities enforcement, and qui tam cases. He is licensed to practice at the state level.
    b. Phone: 415-393-8362
    c. Email: wchan@gibsondunn.com
8. Ernest Hsin at Gibson Dunn, LLC in San Francisco
    a. Hsin works on intellectual property cases, but also works pro bono on cases involving low-income Asians and Asian-Americans. He is licensed to practice at the state level.
    b. Phone: 415-393-8224
    c. Email: ehsin@gibsondunn.com
9. Anthony Bruno at Latham & Watkins, LLC in Los Angeles
    a. Bruno works on finance cases but also pro bono in appellate litigation. He is licensed to practice at both the state and federal level.
    b. Phone: 213-891-8715
    c. Email: Anthony.bruno@lw.com
10. Kasey Branam at Latham & Watkins, LLC in San Diego
    a. Branam works on corporate cases but she works pro bono on fraud litigation and family law cases as well. She is licensed to practice at the state level.
    b. Phone: 858-523-5419
    c. Email: kasey.branam@lw.com

Colorado

1. **Nicholas DeWeese at Hogan Levells, LLC**
    a. DeWeese works on complex civil litigation dn environmental litigation, but he also does pro bono work on immigration, asylum, civil rights,

and criminal defense. He is licensed to practice at the state level.
    b. Phone: 303-454-2530
    c. Email: Nicholas.deweese@hoganlovells.com
2. Colorado Lawyers Committee
    a. This is a consortium of pro bono lawyers working on 'impact litigation.' They typically do not take individual cases but they can connect Justice for Pro Se's clients to lawyers who can take their cases.
    b. Phone: 303-837-1313
3. Robert S. Bruer (See information under 'Kansas')

Connecticut

1. **Pattis & Smith Law Firm**
    a. This firm handles civil rights violations.
    b. Phone: 202-393-3017
    c. Email: information@pattislawfirm.com
2. Spinella & Associates
    a. This firm handles criminal defense.
    b. Phone: 860-728-4900
    c. Email: attorneys@spinella-law.com
3. Robert S. Bruer (See information under 'Kansas')

Delaware

1. Ken Abraham (already committed to Justice for Pro Se's)
2. **Ross Karsnitz from Morris James, LLC**
    a. Karsnitz works on civil litigation including personal injury cases and workers' compensation cases. He used to practice criminal defense for Delaware's Office of Defense Services and he

litigated capital murder cases during that time. He is licensed to practice at the state level.
   b. Phone: 302-856-7158
   c. Email: rkarsnitz@morrisjames.com
3. **Michael G. Owen from Morris James, LLC**
   a. Owen handles personal injury cases. He used to work on criminal cases in the Delaware Attorney General's office. He is licensed to practice at the state level in Delaware, Pennsylvania, and New Jersey.
   b. Phone: 302-651-3583
   c. Email: mowen@morrisjames.com
4. Charles H. Toliver, IV at Morris James, LLC
   a. Toliver now works on alternate dispute resolution but he used to be a Delaware Superior Court judge presiding over civil and criminal cases. He is licensed to practice at the state level.
   b. Phone: 302-888-6941
   c. Email: ctoliver@morrisjames.com
5. David B. Brown at Potter Anderson, LLC
   a. Brown works exclusively on pro bono cases. He chaired a state-wide volunteer lawyer program that provided free legal services to the low-income community of Delaware. He is licensed to practice at the state level for Delaware and also at the federal district level for D.C.
   b. Phone: 302-984-6013
   c. Email: dbrown@potteranderson.com

D.C.

1. Michael McCabe
2. David B. Brown (see his information under 'Delaware')
3. Allison D. Balus (see her information under 'Iowa')

Florida

1. James Cook
2. Florida Justice Institute
    a. This organization works on prisoners' rights.
    b. Phone: 305-358-2081
3. Jacksonville Area Legal Aid Public Service Project
    a. Phone: 904-356-8371

Georgia

1. **Valerie K. Richmond at Stites, LLC**
    a. Richmond works on cases involving banks, but she has also worked at the Atlanta Legal Aid Society on bankruptcy, housing, family law, and other civil matters, and she has also helped the Cobb Justice Foundation, which refers civil matters for Georgia residents to pro bono attorneys throughout the state. She is licensed to practice at the state and federal level for Georgia, Illinois, New York, the Seventh Circuit, the Eleventh Circuit, the Supreme Court).
    b. Phone: 404-739-8814
    c. Email: vrichmond@stites.com
2. Sara Totonchi at the Georgia Center for Human Rights
    a. Totonchi works on prisoners' rights cases and she is also the executive director of the Southern Center for Human Rights.
    b. Email: stotonchi@schr.org
3. Andrea Young at the American Civil Liberties Union of Georgia
    a. Young is the executive director of the American Civil Liberties Union of Georgia.
    b. Email: info@acluga.org

Hawaii

1. **Mark S. Davis at Davis Levin, LLC**
    a. Davis works on civil rights and employment cases. He was on the Board of Directors of the ACLU. He is licensed to practice at the state and federal level.
    b. Phone: 866-806-4349
    c. Email: mdavis@davislevin.com
2. **Joseph Rosenbaum at Fujiwara and Rosenbaum, LLC**
    a. Rosenbaum works on civil rights and employment cases. He was a member of the Hawaii Innocence Project for two years (exonerating prisoners). He is licensed to practice at the state and federal level.
    b. Phone: 808-203-5346
3. Mateo Caballero at the American Civil Liberties Union of Hawaii
    a. Caballero is the legal director at the American Civil Liberties Union of Hawaii.
    b. Phone: 808-522-5908
    c. Email: mcaballero@acluhawaii.org

Idaho

1. **Greg Hampikian**
    a. Hampikian works on post-conviction review for the Idaho Innocence Project. He is licensed to practice at the state level.
    b. Phone: 208-426-4992
2. Idaho Volunteer Lawyers Program
    a. This organization provides legal services for civil cases. You can make contact with them to refer you to pro bono lawyers.
    b. Phone: 208-334-4500

3. Monica Hopkins at the American Civil Liberties Union of Idaho
   a. Hopkins works on prison inmate grievances. She is licensed to practice at the state level.
   b. Phone: 208-334-9750
4. Lea Cooper at the American Civil Liberties Union of Idaho
   a. Cooper works on prison inmate grievances. She is licensed to practice at the state level.
   b. Phone: 208-334-9750 (possibly shares a phone with Hopkins)

Illinois

1. Aknur Shah (already committed to Justice for Pro Se's)
2. Justin Schwartz (already committed to Justice for Pro Se's)
3. Sakina Carbide (already committed to Justice for Pro Se's)
4. **Valerie K. Richmond (See her in 'Georgia')**
5. **Katherine Schon Brockway (See her in 'California')**
6. **Jonathan Little at Saeed & Little, LLC**
   a. Little works on civil rights cases and personal injury cases, particularly for Olympic athletes who were molested by their coaches. You will be meeting with Little in February for a breakfast with other Indiana-area civil rights lawyers. Little is licensed to practice at the state and federal level in Illinois, Indiana, and Arizona.
   b. Phone: 317-721-9214
   c. Email: jon@sllawfirm.com
7. Robert Bruer (See information under 'Kansas')

Indiana

1. Brian Vukadinovich (already committed to Justice for Pro Se's)
2. Jonathan Little (see him in 'Illinois')
3. Neal F. Bailen at Stites, LLC
    a. Bailen works on cases involving financial institutions in consumer litigation but he is the chairman of Southern Indiana Pro Bono Referrals, Inc. He is licensed to practice at the state and federal level in Indiana and Kentucky.
    b. Phone: 812-218-1703
    c. Email: nbailen@stites.com
4. Jessica Wegg at Saeed and Little, LLC
    a. Wegg works on civil rights cases and injury cases. You will be meeting with Wegg in February for a breakfast with other Indiana-area civil rights lawyers. Wegg is licensed to practice in Indiana at the state and federal level.
    b. Phone: 317-721-9214
    c. Email: jessica@sllawfirm.com Iowa

Iowa

1. Allison D. Balus at Baird Holm, LLP
    a. Balus works on Title VII cases, ADA cases, whistleblower cases, discrimination cases, and employment/fair housing cases. She is licensed to practice at the state and federal levels in Iowa, Nebraska, D.C., and Virginia.
    b. Phone: 402-636-8254
    c. Email: abalus@bairdholm.com
2. Marina Grabchuk at Belin McCormick
    a. Grabchuk works on immigration cases, but she has done much pro bono work on civil rights

(mostly employment cases). She is licensed to practice at the state level.
  - b. Phone: 515-283-4635
  - c. Email: msgrabchuk@belinmccormick.com
3. Rita Betis at the American Civil Liberties Union of Iowa
   - a. Betis works on civil rights and litigation involving prison conditions. She works mostly on 'impact' cases, but she will take on some one-off prisoner cases. She probably knows everyone in the community doing this kind of work in Iowa.
   - b. Phone: 515-243-3988
   - c. Email: rita.bettis@aclu-ia.org
4. Robert S. Bruer (See information under 'Kansas')

Kansas

1. **Robert S. Bruer at Bruer Law Firm, LLC**
   - a. Bruer works on personal injury cases. He is licensed to practice in Kansas and Missouri at the state and federal levels. He is also licensed to practice in Colorado, Connecticut, Illinois, Iowa, and Nevada at the state level.
   - b. Phone: 816-912-0030
   - c. Email: rob@bruerlaw.com
2. Christopher Joseph at Joseph, Hollander, & Craft, LLC
   - a. Joseph works on bank fraud cases, drug crimes, pornography prosecutions, and related civil matters including complex civil litigation in federal court. Joseph is licensed to practice at the state and federal level.
   - b. Phone: 785-234-3272
   - c. Email: cjoseph@josephhollander.com

Kentucky

1. **Neal F. Bailen at Stites & Harbison (see information in 'Indiana')**
2. Rebecca McKelvey Castaneda at Stites & Harbison
    a. Castaneda works on family law cases including international family law involving parental child abductions. She is licensed to practice at the state level for Kentucky and at the state and federal level for Tennessee.
    b. Phone: 617-782-2204
    c. Email: Rebecca.mckelvey@stites.com

Louisiana

1. Laura Caviness at Curry Caviness & Webb
    a. Caviness works on environmental and tort litigation. She is licensed to practice at the state level.
    b. Phone: 504-524-8556
    c. Email: lcaviness@ccw-lawfirm.com

Maine

1. Edward Blum (Already committed to Justice for Pro Se's)
2. **Maine Prisoner Advocacy Coalition**
    a. This organization works on prisoners' rights and connects attorneys with prisoners.
    b. Email: maineprisoneradvocacy@yahoo.com
3. Alison Beyes at the American Civil Liberties Union of Maine
    a. Beyes is the Executive Director of the American Civil Liberties Union of Maine.
    b. Email: info@mclu.org

Maryland

1. William Bond (works with Posner—technically not a member of the company)
2. Michael McCabe (already committed to Justice for Pro Se's)
3. James Geiser (already committed to Justice for Pro Se's)

Massachusetts

1. Charles Blackman (already committed to Justice for Pro Se's)
2. **Eleanor Hertzberg at Eleanor R. Hertzberg Law**
    a. Hertzberg works on criminal defense and a large portion of her work involves pro bono work with young men and women charged with drug offenses. Theresa used to work for her and recommends her highly. She also runs a directory of pro bono lawyers involved with the Massachusetts Drug Court. She is licensed to practice at the state level in Massachusetts and New York.
    b. Phone: 978-800-1872
    c. Email: erh8@cornell.edu
3. Amanda L. Vanderhorst
    a. Vanderhorst works on family law cases. Jesse Hogin recommends her personally. She is licensed to practice at the state level.
    b. Phone: 617-412-4206
    c. Email: avanderhorst@katesbarlow.com

Michigan

1. **David Nacht at Nacht Law**
   a. Nacht works on civil rights cases and criminal law. He is licensed to practice at the state and federal level.
   b. Phone: 734-418-0356
   c. Email: dnacht@nachtlaw.com
2. **Michael J. Steinberg at the American Civil Liberties Union of Michigan**
   a. Steinberg is the legal director of the American Civil Liberties Union of Michigan.
   b. Phone: 313-578-6800
   c. Email: msteinberg@aclumich.org
3. **Dean Elliot at Dean Elliot, PLC**
   a. Elliot works on civil rights and commercial litigation. He is licensed to practice at both the state and federal level.
   b. Phone: 248-251-0001
   c. Email: dean@deanelliottplc.com

Minnesota

1. **Tom Kramer at Kramer Law Offices**
   a. Kramer works on indigents' cases pro bono. Kramer is licensed to practice at the state level.
   b. Phone: 507-828-0594
   c. Email: attorney@kramerlawoffice.net
2. Briggs & Morgan Law Firm
   a. This firm works on indigents' cases pro bono.
   b. Phone: 612-977-8400
3. Larry McDowell
   a. Larry McDowell works on indigents' cases pro bono. McDowell is licensed to practice at the state level.
   b. Phone: 218-681-3111

Mississippi

1. **Claire W. Ketner**
    a. Ketner works on commercial litigation cases, personal injury cases, and labor/employment cases. She is also part of the Mississippi Volunteer Lawyers' Project and the Defense Lawyers Association. She is licensed to practice at the state and federal level.
    b. Phone: 601-973-8714
    c. Email: cketner@brunini.com
2. **R. Lane Bobo at Brunini**
    a. Bobo works on medical malpractice cases but also is a member of the Mississippi Defense Lawyers Association. He also volunteers with the Catholic Charities' Immigration Clinic. He is licensed to practice at the state level.
    b. Phone: 601-960-6852
    c. Email: lbobo@bunini.com

Missouri

1. **Michael Foster at Polsinelli**
    a. Foster works on commercial litigation cases but he recently won a high-profile prisoners' rights case. He is licensed to practice at the state level in Missouri.
    b. Email: mfoster@polsinelli.com
2. **Philip Zeeck at Polsinelli**
    a. Zeeck, similar to Foster, works on commercial litigation cases, but he recently won a high-profile prisoners' rights case. He is licensed to practice at the state level in Missouri.
    b. Phone: 816-572-4592
    c. Email: pzeeck@polsinelli.com

3. Robert Sills at Orrick
    a. Sills works on complex litigation and arbitration, but he was a lead partner on a pro bono team challenging inadequate public defense. He is licensed to practice at the state level in New York and Missouri.
    b. Phone: 212-506-5110
    c. Email: rsills@orrick.com
4. Robert S. Bruer (see information in 'Kansas')

Montana

1. **McCallister Law Firm**
    a. This firm works on civil rights cases.
    b. Phone: 816-931-2229
2. Peter Wagner at the Prison Policy Initiative
    a. Wagner is the executive director of the Prison Policy Initiative and he works on civil rights cases.
    b. Mail: Prison Policy Initiative, PO Box 127, Northampton, MA 01061

Nebraska

1. **Allison D. Balus at Baird Holm, LLP (See information in 'Iowa')**
2. Sean T. Nakamoto at Baird Holm, LLP
    a. Nakamoto works on healthcare/health insurance cases. He is licensed to practice at the state level.
    b. Phone: 402-636-8247
    c. Email: snakamoto@bairdholm.com
3. Jerry Hug at Stoler Hug Law
    a. Hug works on criminal defense cases for white-collar crimes and drug offenses. He is licensed to practice at the state level.

b. Phone: 402-346-1733
c. Website: http://www.stolerhuglaw.com
4. Alan Stoler at Stoler Hug Law
   a. Stoler works on criminal defenses for white-collar crimes and drug offenses. He is licensed to practice at the state level.
   b. Phone: 402-346-1733
   c. Website: http://www.stolerhuglaw.com

Nevada

1. Robert R. Bauer (see information in 'Kansas')
2. Barbara Buckley at the Legal Aid Clinic of Southern Nevada
   a. Buckley is the executive director of the Legal Aid Clinic of Southern Nevada
   b. Phone: 702-386-1070
3. Noah Malgeri
   a. Malgeri works on the Pro Bono Project for the Legal Aid Clinic of Southern Nevada.
   b. Phone: 702-386-1070 (same as Buckley's above)

New Hampshire

1. Pamela A. Peterson
   a. Peterson works on family law cases but she is a partner of a New Hampshire Firm that volunteers with a pro bono referral program.
   b. Phone: 603-695-8655
   c. Email: ppeterson@devinemillimet.com
2. Giles Bissonnette at the American Civil Liberties Union of New Hampshire
   a. Bissonnette is the legal director for ACLU New Hampshire.

b. Website: https://www.aclu-nh.org/en/email/node/392/field_bio_email

New Jersey

1. **Paul A. Clark at Paul Clark Legal**
   a. Clark is a former Posner clerk and a University of Chicago Law graduate. He now works in criminal defense. He is licensed to practice at the state and federal level.
   b. Phone: 202-368-5435
   c. Email: pclark@pclarklegal.com
2. **Edward Barocas at American Civil Liberties Union of New Jersey**
   a. Barocas is the legal director for the American Civil Liberties Union of New Jersey.
   b. Phone: 973-642-6253
   c. Email: ebarocas@aclu-nj.org

New Mexico

1. **John Harrington at Holland & Hart**
   a. Harrington works on civil rights cases and defense of low-income clients.
   b. Phone: 801-799-1922
2. New Mexico Legal Aid
   a. This group works on civil legal assistance, but only on non-criminal matters.
   b. Phone: 866-416-1922

New York

1. Katherine Macfarlane (Already committed to Justice for Pro Se's)
2. Eleanor Hertzberg (See information under 'Massachusetts')
3. Valerie K. Richmond (See information under 'Georgia')
4. Diana Aguilar (See information under 'California')
5. Jonathan Little (See information under 'Illinois')

North Carolina

1. Claire Rauscher at Womble, Bond, & Dickinson
    a. Rauscher worked for over 25 years on criminal justice defense. She now works with corporate clients. She is licensed to practice at the state and federal level in North Carolina and at the state level in Pennsylvania.
    b. Phone: 704-331-4961
    c. Email: Claire.rauscher@wbd-us.com
2. Debbie W. Harden at Womble, Bond, & Dickinson
    a. Harden works on business litigation including ERISA cases. She is licensed to practice at the state and federal level.
    b. Phone: 704-331-4943
    c. Email: Debbie.harden@wbd-us.com
3. Brian Hayles at Womble, Bond, & Dickinson
    a. Hayles works on antitrust cases but he also works pro bono for veterans' cases. He is licensed to practice at the state and federal level in North Carolina and at the state level in South Carolina.
    b. Phone: 704-331-4961
    c. Email: brian.hayles@wbd-us.com

4. Alysja S. Carlisle at Womble, Bond, & Dickinson
   a. Carlisle works on antitrust cases but she is also on the council for ABA Section of Civil Rights and Social Justice. She is licensed to practice at the state and federal level.
   b. Phone: 704-350-6362
   c. Email: alysja.carlisle@wbd-us.com

North Dakota

1. Sandra Freeman
   a. Freeman works on Indian law and water rights. She represents the DAPL protestors. It appears that the entire North Dakota pro bono community is swamped with work from the DAPL protests.
   b. Phone: 703-254-3402

Ohio

1. **Brian D. Joslyn of Joslyn Law Firm**
   a. Joslyn works on criminal defense cases. He was a victim of police brutality after a police officer split his skull open after hitting him with a flashlight and then stomped on his body. This experience led to Joslyn's pursuit of the law. He is licensed to practice at the state level.
   b. Phone: 614-444-1900
2. Benjamin Luftman at Luftman, Heck, & Associates
   a. Luftman works on criminal defense cases. He is licensed to practice at the state level.
   b. Phone: 614-962-6076
   c. Email: advice@columbuscriminalattorney.com

3. Vicevich Law
    a. This firm specializes in civil litigation.
    b. Phone: 406-782-1111

Oklahoma

1. **Anthony Hendricks at Crowe & Dunlevy**
    a. Hendricks works on white-collar criminal defense cases. He is a former Marshall Scholar at the London School of Economics. He is licensed to practice at the state and federal level.
    b. Phone: 405-239-5411
    c. Email: Anthony.hendricks@crowedunlevy.com
2. Elizabeth Bowersox at Mcafee Taft
    a. Bowersox works on labor and employment cases. She is licensed to practice at the state and federal level.
    b. Phone: 405-270-6019
    c. Email: Elizabeth.bowersox@mcafeetaft.com
3. Maggie J. Dowdy at Crowe & Dunlevy
    a. Dowdy works on criminal defense cases, environmental cases, and energy cases. She is licensed to practice at the state level.
    b. Phone: 405-239-6687
    c. Email: Maggie.dowdy@crowedunlevy.com

Oregon

1. **Owen D. Blank at Tonkon Torp, LLP**
    a. Blank works on cases involving small businesses, nonprofits, and sports law. He has worked for almost 20 years providing pro bono legal services at a nonprofit called Albina Head Start that serves thousands of children and their

families. He is licensed to practice at the state and federal level in Oregon.
    b. Phone: 503-802-2011
    c. Email: owen.blank@tonkon.com
2. Meg Houlihan at Tonkon Torp, LLP
    a. Houlihan works on business cases involving contracts and commercial disputes, but she used to work on cases involving tenant evictions. She is licensed to practice at the state level.
    b. Phone: 503-802-2184
    c. Email: meg.houlihan@tonkon.com

Pennsylvania

1. **Stephen D. Brown at Dechert**
    a. Brown works on civil rights cases and maintains an active pro bono practice. Brown is licensed to practice at the state level.
    b. Phone: 215-994-2240
    c. Email: Stephen.brown@dechert.com
2. **Claire Rauscher (See information in 'North Carolina')**
3. Pennsylvania Institutional Rights Project
    a. This organization works on prisoner rights and serves pro se's.
    b. Phone: 215-925-2966
    c. Email: alove@pailp.org
4. Reggie Shuford at the American Civil Liberties Union of Pennsylvania
    a. Shuford is the executive director of the ACLU of Pennsylvnia.

Puerto Rico

1. Evan M. Migdail at DLA Piper
    a. Migdail represents corporations and he recently represented the government of Puerto Rico for a major expansion of its healthcare system under the Affordable Care Act. He is licensed to practice in D.C. and Maryland.
    b. Phone: 202-799-4311
    c. Email: evan.migdail@dlapiper.com
2. Puerto Rico Legal Services, Inc.
    a. This organization provides free legal representation to poor Puerto Ricans in civil cases. It works on civil rights cases, consumer/debt/credit/bankruptcy cases, elder law, education cases, employment cases, family and juvenile cases, housing and health cases, and veterans' litigation.
    b. Phone: 787-728-8686
    c. Email: communicaciones@servicioslegales.org

Rhode Island

1. **Thomas W. Lyons III**
    a. Lyons works on civil litigation and constitutional law cases. He leads a firm with a pro bono civil rights practice. He is licensed to practice at the state and federal level.
    b. Phone: 401-400-4416
    c. Email: tlyons@sfandllaw.com
2. Mark Dana at Dana and Dana
    a. Dana works on criminal cases. He is licensed to practice at the state and federal level.
    b. Phone: 401-232-4004
    c. Email: info@danaanddana.com

South Carolina

1. Deborah Davis (Already committed to Justice for Pro Se's)
2. **Brian Hayles (See information in 'North Carolina')**
3. John Blume
    a. Blume is a professor at Cornell Law School who works on death penalty appeals.
    b. Phone: 607-255-1030
    c. Email: jp94@cornell.edu
4. Robert B. King, Jr. at Thompson and King
    a. King works on criminal defense cases and domestic law.
    b. Phone: 864-769-0112
5. South Carolina Appleseed
    a. This organization provides legal services for veterans.
    b. Phone: 803-779-1113
    c. Email: info@scjustice.org

South Dakota

1. **Kathryn J. Hoskins at Bangs McCullen**
    a. Hoskins works on civil jury trials. She also worked full-time as a critical care nurse before and during law school. Her medical knowledge could be useful for cases about prisoners' conditions. She is licensed to practice at the state level.
    b. Phone: 605-339-6800
2. Eric J. Pickar at Bangs McCullen
    a. Pickar works on civil rights cases and criminal defense cases. Pickar is licensed to practice at the state level.
    b. Phone: 605-343-1040

Tennessee

1. Rebecca McKelvey Castaneda (See information in 'Kentucky')
2. R. Andrew Free practices in Nashville; his practice incudes immigration law and police accountability (but is not limited to those fields), and he is admitted to practice in four federal courts of appeals and five federal district courts.
3. Ryan T. Holt also practices in Nashville. His focus is business litigation in a variety of industries, but he has also litigated habeas corpus and received a pro bono service award from the Tennessee Supreme Court.
4. Charles Silvestri Higgins practices in Memphis, with emphasis on personal injury litigation, including medical malpractice.
5. Ashley N. Goins at Stites & Harbison
   a. Goins works on business litigation cases, but she also won the Tennessee Supreme Court's 2017 Pro Bono Service Award. She is licensed to practice at the state and federal level.
   b. Phone: 615-782-2311
   c. Email: agoins@stites.com
6. Byron N. Brown IV at Wyatt, Tarrant, and Combs, LLP
   a. Brown works on commercial civil litigation and white-collar criminal defense but he recently represented a state prisoner in a federal civil rights action. He is licensed to practice at both the state and federal levels.
   b. Phone: 901-537-1038
   c. Email: bbrown@wyattfirm.com
7. Baker Donelson (law firm)
   a. This firm appears to have a brisk pro bono practice.
   b. Phone: 423-756-2010 (for Chattanooga office) and 865-549-7000 (for Knoxville office) and 423-

928-0181 (for Johnson City office) and 901-526-2000 (for Memphis office) and 901-579-3100 (for Memphis east office)

Texas

1. Chris Ogolla (Already committed to Justice for Pro Se's)
2. **Loren E. Weiss at Ray Quinney & Nebeker**
    a. Weiss works on antitrust cases, whistleblower cases, and white-collar criminal defense. She is also a board member of the Rocky Mountain Innocence Center. She is licensed to practice at the state level.
    b. Phone: 801-323-3330
    c. Email: lweiss@rqn.com
3. **Scott Medlock at Edwards Law**
    a. Medlock works on jail abuse cases. He is licensed to practice at the state level.
    b. Phone: 512-623-7727
    c. Email: jeff@edwards-law.com
4. Texas Civil Rights Project (Prisoners' Rights Program)
    a. The organization works on criminal justice within the state of Texas.
    b. Phone: 512-474-5073
    c. Email: info@texascivilrightsproject.org
5. The Habern Law Firm
    a. The firm works on criminal defense. Its lawyers are licensed to practice within the state of Texas.
    b. Phone: 713-942-2376
    c. Email: info@paroletexas.com

Utah

1. **Amy F. Sorenson at Snell & Wilmer**
    a. Sorenson works on commercial litigation cases

but she is the president of the board of directors at the Legal Aid Society of Salt Lake City. She is licensed to practice at the state and federal level.
    b. Phone: 801-257-1907
    c. Email: asorenson@swlaw.com
2. Katherine E. Priest at Ray Quinney & Nebeker
    a. Priest works on white-collar/corporate compliance but she used to teach police cadets about criminal and civil law issues at a police academy. She is licensed to practice at the state level.
    b. Phone: 801-323-3390
    c. Email: krpiest@rqn.com

Vermont

1. Angele Court at the Vermont Volunteer Lawyers Project
    a. Phone: 802-863-7153
2. Margaret Frye at Law Line of Vermont
    a. Phone: 802-863-7153 (same as Angele Court's)

Virginia

1. Michael McCabe (Already committed to Justice for Pro Se's)
2. Allison D. Baird (See information in 'Iowa')
3. Kim Macleod at Hunter & Williams
    a. Macleod works on corporate cases. She is recommended by Steven Hazel.
    b. Phone: 804-788-8529
    c. Email: kmacleod@hunton.com
4. Mary Anne Stone at Virginia Citizens United for the Rehabilitation of Errants
    a. Stone is the president of the Virginia Citizens United for the Rehabilitation of Errants.

b. Phone: 703-272-3624
   c. Email: mary.anne.stone@verizon.net

Washington

1. **Philip Buri at Buri Funston**
   a. Buri works on appeals and civil matters. He comes recommended by your UMichigan RA, Jesse Hogin. He is a former clerk of a U.S. district court and the Washington Supreme Court, and a Harvard Law alum. He is licensed to practice at the state and federal level.
   b. Phone: 360-752-1500
   c. Email: Philip@burifunston.com
2. **Salvaor A. Mungia**
   a. Mungia works on civil litigation cases, but he also works pro bono on cases involving prisoner litigation. He is licensed to practice at both the state and federal level.
   b. Phone: 253-620-6472
   c. Email: smungia@gth-law.com
3. **Emily Chiang at American Civil Liberties Union of Washington**
   a. Chiang is a Harvard law alum and now leading the ACLU Washington office. She is also a former law professor from the University of Utah.
   b. Phone: 206-624-2184
   c. Email: echiang@aclu-wa.org
4. **Phil Talmadge at Tal Fitzlaw**
   a. Talmadge works on appeals and is a former Washington Supreme Court justice. He is licensed to practice at both the state and federal level.
   b. Phone: 206-574-6661
   c. Email: phil@tal-fitzlaw.com

West Virginia

1. **James F. Companion at Schrader, Byrd, & Companion**
   a. Companion works on civil matters and the treatment of prison inmates. He is licensed to practice at the state level.
   b. Phone: 304-233-3390
   c. Email: jfc@schraderlaw.com
2. Fazal A. Shere at Bowles Rice
   a. Shere works on civil matters and the defense of indigent clients. He is licensed to practice at the state level.
   b. Phone: 304-347-1709
3. Legal Aid of West Virginia
   a. This organization works only on civil matters in the state of West Virginia.
   b. Phone: 866-255-4370

Wisconsin

1. Aknur Shah (already committed to Justice for Pro Se's)
2. **Lisa M. Amundson at DeWitt Ross & Stevens**
   a. Amundson works in family law, and she is a pro bono lawyer for a Wisconsin legal aid group. She is licensed to practice at the state level.
   b. Phone: 612-305-1407
   c. Email: lxa@dewittmcm.com
3. **Lindsey M. Anderson at DeWitt, Ross, & Stevens**
   a. Anderson works on family law, trademarks, and litigation. She is also a pro bono lawyer for crime victims. She is licensed to practice at the state level.
   b. Phone: 262-754-2857
   c. Email: lma@dewittross.com

4. Kathryn L. Farnsworth at DeWitt, Ross, & Stevens
    a. Farnsworth works on personal injury cases. She also worked for the Wisconsin Innocence Project. She is licensed to practice at the state level.
    b. Phone: 608-754-2857
    c. Email: klf@dewittross.com

Wyoming

1. Stephen Pevar at the American Civil Liberties Union
    a. Pevar works on Indian law and prisoner litigation. He is not based on Wyoming, but he takes an interest in the Big Sky region and has represented ACLU in several Wyoming cases.
    b. Email: Stephen.pevar@nyu.edu
2. Equal Justice Wyoming
    a. This nonprofit coordinates pro bono legal services. It does not directly represent anyone. It is likely to have contact information based on Justice for Pro Se's referrals.
    b. Phone: 307-777-8383
    c. Email: wcla@legalhelpwy.org

The Mission of My Company: A Statement

Goals

1. To match pro se litigants who have meritorious cases to *pro bono* lawyers, sometimes to other lawyers, sometimes to nonlawyers.
2. To train litigants to advocate for themselves without a lawyer.
3. To encourage lawyers and other members of Justice for Pro Se's to work with poor or desperate people, prison inmates, and other individuals whom they normally would avoid in a legal practice.

A Note on History

The company was created in the fall of 2017 by me, Richard A. Posner, who after 35 and 2/3 years as a judge of the Court of Appeals for the Seventh Circuit realized belatedly that the judges of his court were disserving pro se litigants. This realization induced me to retire from the court, which I did on September 2, 2017. As I then began speaking and writing about the pro se issue (notably, *Improving the Federal Judiciary*, published on December 4, 2017), I received requests from a number of prisoner and other pro se's who needed assistance in their cases. I also received offers of support from a number of lawyers who expressed interest in leveling the legal playing field for pro se's. Recognizing my status as a hub connecting the two groups, I founded this company to address the national mismatch between poor individuals and the lawyers who could, but currently do not, help them, and I was induced to expand the firm to its present, growing size.

A Note on Company Structure

My company, which as I have noted is nonprofit, is, as noted earlier in the book, about to be reorganized as a 501(c)(3) company. (See Google entry 501 c 3 nonprofit organization.) Donations to such a company are exempt from taxes—a feature that encourages donations. The firm's headquarters are in Chicago, but the firm is active in many states and aims to be active in all of them, as well as in offshore U.S. territories, such as Puerto Rico and Guam. The firm is primarily a free referral service, matching pro se's with lawyers and non-lawyers to help on their cases.

I am the sole owner of the company but now have a board of directors to assist me with its governance. All members of the firm (at present more than 80 including me and the company's at present only consultant (Jennifer Nou), and the company's research director, Theresa Yuan, whose staff consists of six University of Chicago law students and one University of Chicago college senior, provide as much assistance to the firm's pro se clientele as is consistent with their interest in the firm's goals and activities and their available time.

The firm's members are not employees, are not salaried, instead are volunteer helpers, but they will be compensated for outstanding performance. Those who are lawyers will be responsible for their own malpractice insurance, will be able to count hours spent on cases for my company toward their state bar's pro bono hour requirements, and may report their participation in my company to their firm. Nonlawyers who have extensive experience advising and/or litigating matters on behalf of themselves or pro se's will be invited to work with individuals who have meritorious cases that do not require a lawyer's guidance. The company's lawyers and nonlawyers alike often are able to teach pro se's to litigate their cases themselves—to be in effect their own courtroom lawyers. And it bears repetition that as I emphasized earlier in this book, Justice for Pro Se's aspires eventually to have legal representatives in every state and every foreign possession of the United States.

Some lawyers who have volunteered time to my company are unable to represent any pro se's because of law-firm obligations or other work obligations, such as teaching. These lawyers will serve in an advisory capacity, as consultants, commenting on latest developments via email. Contractors will sometimes be needed, such as George Rumsey, a computer expert (in fact a techy genius) who both is a member of my company and has helped me enormously with my recent books—including of course this book. There will be as mentioned a board of directors, and donations will be solicited.

Regional Direction

As the firm expands, the need for subdividing direction grows; and I have decided therefore to appoint from within the company a series of Regional Directors, each of whom will supervise my company's operations in a contiguous (generally multistate) area. I have appointed Jonathan Zell to be the first Regional Director; his domain will be Ohio (where he lives and works), Michigan, Kentucky, and West Virginia. The second

Regional Director I've appointed is Sakina Carbide, a first-rate Chicago lawyer; her region will be the City of Chicago. Third is Matthew Dowd, a Washington, D.C. lawyer who has agreed to be the Regional Director for Washington, D.C. plus the states of the Fourth Circuit (Maryland, Virginia, North Carolina and South Carolina) other than West Virginia, assigned as just mentioned to Zell. Brian Vukadinovich will be the Regional Director for Indiana (where he resides) and Illinois south of Chicago; that is the region of Illinois that abuts Indiana.

The specific responsibilities of the Regional Directors will include the following:

As you are the Regional Director of Region # (state the # of the region) we would like to ask you to provide some information to us in order that we will be able to ascertain the progress of our company and to ensure that we are having a positive impact in meeting the goals of our mission in helping needy pro se's. We realize that you are busy and that your time is valuable, so we are making an effort to make this reporting process as least cumbersome as possible. We would like to have a monthly update to keep track of the progress of things in each Region. As part of your responsibilities as Regional Director of (state the region) we are hopeful that you will maintain contact with each of the members of our company in your region, monitor the progress of each of them, and cultivate contacts with lawyers, law firms, pro bono organizations, and pro se's in your region. Attached to this message is a report form that we would like you to utilize in submitting the information to us. We ask that you provide a monthly report. If you have any questions or concerns please do not hesitate to contact one or both us. Thank you for being a valuable member of our company in carrying out its mission of helping pro se's. We very much appreciate it.

Dick Posner and Brian Vukadinovich

REGIONAL DIRECTOR REPORT

Region #:_____

1. Please state the efforts you have made to be in contact with members in your region in monitoring the progress of the individual members in terms of their contributions in helping pro se's with their cases.

2. Please state the names of members of your region who have actively assisted pro se's in helping fulfill the mission of Justice for Pro Se's.

3. Please state the individual cases that members have assisted pro se's, i.e., civil case, criminal case, issues of case, nature of assistance, i.e., advice, representation, etc.

4. Please state the members of your region who have not assisted any pro se's in any manner.

5. Please state your efforts in maintaining contact with each member of your region inmonitoring the progress of each member in your region.

6. Please state your efforts in recruiting potential members in your region that would be willing to volunteer to Justice for Pro Se's either as an attorney or lay member to help pro se's by either representing pro se's or providing guidance.

7. Please state your efforts in maintaining relations with the leading law firms and lawyers in your district in learning as much as possible about the pro se's in your

district and any efforts you have made in sharing information with other pro bono organizations.

Report Submitted by:

_____

Director of Region # _____

Date of Report:_____

A recent addition to the company is Bradley Fuller, a very able and experienced Chicago lawyer. I have made him Regional Director for the area north of the Chicago River to and including Milwaukee, Wisconsin. Since the Chicago River bisects the City of Chicago, his region will overlap that of Sakina Carbide, but I see no problem in joint direction of the relatively small area between the Chicago River and the northern limit of the City of Chicago where both Carbide and Fuller practice law.

I emphasized to Mr. Fuller that I do not require anyone whom we hire to work full time for my company, for many of them are committed to devote substantial to their own practice, often as the member of a law firm. I am content if the person whom I hire is willing to devote at least several hours a month to pro se's whom we can steer to him, who can also scout his territory for pro se's in need of professional assistance, and finally who can keep tabs on other pro bono lawyers in his territory who might be recruited to my company, again on a part-time basis. Mr. Fuller meets all these requirements.

Expert litigator Alan Popkin of St. Louis has agreed to be our Regional Director for his state (Missouri) and maybe others, such as Tennessee and Iowa. I have discussed with superlawyer James V. Cook of Florida his willingness to be our Regional Director in that state and also in Georgia and Alabama. Unfortunately Mr. Cook has declined my invitation and as a result I am looking for a substitute Regional Director for those three states. As it happens, a large, distinguished, nationwide law firm named Polsinelli has a large presence in Atlanta, which happens to be both the capital of Georgia and the state's most populous city. I am in touch with two of Polsinelli's very impressive lawyers, Michael Foster and Michelle Clardy, and though they are in Polsinelli's Kansas City office, I am hoping that they will enable me to recruit one of the firm's lawyers in Atlanta to be the regional director of a region consisting of Georgia, Florida, and Alabama. In addition, Polsinelli's very large practice in Kansas City (250 lawyers!) may enable me to obtain regional directors for states to the west of Kansas—states such as Colorado in which Polsinelli is already active. Accommodation of the contribution that Polsinelli can make to my company may require some adjustment of already existing regions of my company in those states.

I asked my former law clerk Aaron Van Oort, a deservedly very successful lawyer in Minneapolis and a member of Justice for Pro Se's, to take over a region consisting of Wisconsin, Minnesota, and North and South Dakota. Unfortunately he has declined. I have not heard back yet from Amanda Vanderhorst, a Boston lawyer, member of my company, whom I have invited to become Regional Director for New England.

Patrick Thesing has volunteered to be our Regional Director in Texas (where he lives), plus—hold your breath—in either 14 or 16 other states (wow!), in the Fifth, Eighth, and Tenth Federal Circuits. The states are: Fifth Circuit: Texas, Louisiana, Mississippi. Eighth Circuit: Arkansas, Iowa, Minnesota, Missouri, Nebraska, North Dakota, South Dakota. Tenth Circuit: Colorado, Kansas, New Mexico, Oklahoma, Utah, Wyoming. That's fine with a few minor exceptions, beginning with Missouri, however, which will go mainly to Alan Popkin, as mentioned, but Western Missouri, also some portions of Kansas, will go to Robert Bruer, a new member of Justice for Pro Se's.

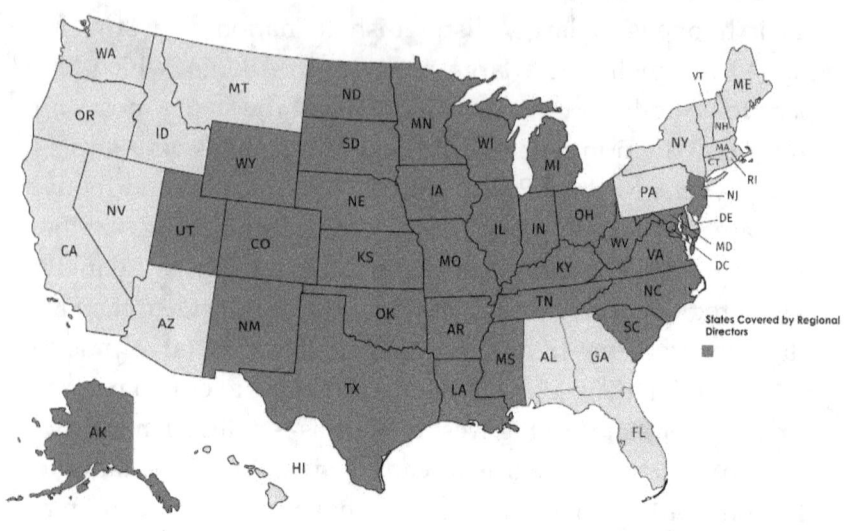

I attach a map of the United States similar to that on page 21, except that the dark areas denote regions in which I have or hope soon to have Regional Directors.

I invite company members to indicate to me states or groups of states, or even just parts of a state or states, that they'd like to be Regional Directors of. I feel a particular sense of urgency with regard to the far west. I envision a region, requiring a director, starting in and running from New Mexico and Arizona to California and thence to Oregon and Washington, but stopping short of Alaska; Paul Clark has accepted appointment as Regional Director of a region consisting of New Jersey and Alaska, because he practices law in both states despite the distance between them.

I may have to create a committee, including directors and consultants, to assist me in choosing the additional Regional Directors who are needed. For I want the Regional Directorships eventually to embrace the entire nation.

A vital role of the Regional Directors is to work with law firms and lawyers in the directors' states in an effort to induce some of them to join my company, emphasizing to them that their membership in the company will not require them to give up their current practice but merely to supplement it to a limited extent. (Indeed, Sonja Ebron of Courtroom5, whose company so resembles mine, has agreed to become a member of my company.) My goal of course is to provide as much legal assistance as the nation's pro se's—a very considerable group of needy persons—require. To achieve that goal will probably require me to appoint company representatives in every state, as well as every other U.S. territory.

The Regional Directors and other representatives of my company will enjoy considerable autonomy, but should bear in mind that they are ultimately subject to review and supervision by Mr. Vukadinovich and me.

Finally, I intend to hold conferences attended by both Regional Directors and company volunteers.

Here Is a Partial List of Volunteers Sorted under Regional Directors

1. **Region 1 (Jonathan Zell): Ohio, Michigan, Kentucky, West Virginia**
    1. Gary Peeples (Kentucky)
2. **Region 2 (Sakina Carbide): City of Chicago**
    1. Aknur Shah (Illinois)
    2. George Rumsey (Illinois)
    3. Pamela McKinney (Illinois)
    4. Eric Posner (Illinois)
    5. Theresa Yuan (Illinois)
    6. William Landes (Illinois)
    7. Justin Schwartz (Illinois)

3. **Region 3 (Matthew Dowd): Washington, D.C., Maryland, Virginia, North Carolina, South Carolina**
    1. Deborah Davis (South Carolina)
    2. Gregory Sidak (Washington, D.C.)
    3. James Geiser (Maryland)
    4. Shon Hopwood (Washington, D.C.)
    5. Sonja Ebron (North Carolina)
4. **Region 4 (Brian Vukadinovich): Indiana, Illinois (except for Chicago)**
    1. Alan Frankel (Illinois)
    2. Daniel Johnson (Illinois)
    3. James Dawson (Illinois)
    4. Richard Porter (Illinois)
    5. Bryan Birnie (Illinois)
    6. Julia Schwartz (Illinois)
5. **Region 5 (Alan Popkin): Missouri, Tennessee?**
    1. Bruce Hopkins (Missouri)
    2. Rachel Sachs (Missouri)
    3. Phillip Zeeck (Missouri)
    4. Michael Foster (Missouri)
6. **Region 6 (Patrick Thesing): Texas, Louisiana, Mississippi, Arkansas, Iowa, Minnesota, Nebraska, North Dakota, South Dakota, Colorado, New Mexico, Oklahoma, Utah, Wyoming**
    1. Christopher Ogolla (Texas)
    2. Judge John Kane (Colorado)
    3. Robert Sanford (Nebraska)
7. **Region 7 (Robert Bruer): Kansas, Western Missouri**
8. **Region 8 (Paul Clark): New Jersey, Alaska**
9. **Region 9 (Bradley Fuller): territory north of the Chicago River to and including Milwaukee**

10. **Region 10 (Stephen Abeyta): Florida, Alabama, Georgia**
    1. Eric Segall (Georgia)
    2. Gordon Smith (Florida)
    3. James Cook (Florida)

11. **Region 11 (Possible region, if Aaron Van Oort agrees): Wisconsin, Minnesota, North Dakota, South Dakota**
    1. Aaron Van Oort (Minnesota)

12. **Region 12 (Possible region, if Amanda Vanderhorst agrees): Massachusetts, Maine, Vermont, New Hampshire, Rhode Island, Connecticut**
    1. Charles Blackman (Rhode Island)
    2. Brandon Sample (Vermont)
    3. Amanda Vanderhorst (Massachusetts)
    4. Abbe Gluck (Connecticut)
    5. Edward Blum (Maine)
    6. Lawrence Lessig (Massachusetts)

13. **Region 13 (No regional director assigned yet): New Mexico, Arizona, California, Oregon, Washington**
    1. Daniel Klerman (California)
    2. Larry Downes (California)
    3. Rebecca Stone (California)
    4. Thomas Gorman (California)

14. **Volunteers without directors:**
    1. Carito Calvachil-Mateyko (Delaware)
    2. Charles Silvestri Higgins (Tennessee)
    3. Devon Jacob (Pennsylvania)
    4. Eli Jacobs (New York)
    5. Janet Carter (New York)
    6. Ken Abraham (Delaware)
    7. Matthew Freda (Tennessee)

8. R. Andrew Free (Tennessee)
9. Ryan Holt (Tennessee)
10. Shana Pollak (Nevada)

To get a better sense of Regional Direction, we asked one of the directors, Matthew Dowd of Region 3, to provide us with some information in order to help us ascertain the progress of our company and ensure that we are having a positive impact in meeting the goals of our mission of helping pro se's. We realize that you're busy and your time is valuable, so we'll make the reporting process as simple as possible.

We would like a monthly update to keep track of the progress of each Region. As part of your responsibilities as Director of Region 3, you should endeavor to maintain contact with each of the company's volunteers in your region, monitor their progress, and report on their progress or lack thereof to us.

If you have any questions or concerns, please do not hesitate to contact one of us. Thank you for contributing to our company in helping pro se's. We greatly appreciate it.

Dick Posner and Brian Vukadinovich

Intake Revisited

I want to amplify my rather sparse earlier discussion of intake. Cases come to me and other members of my company in phone calls, emails, letters, or a website intake form. Some prisoner cases will also come referred by judges seeking a pro bono lawyer. Intake and case-screening will be carried out like medical triage on a war-torn beach; that is, the pro se's who have obviously good cases and ample resources to litigate will be ignored in favor of the pro se's with good cases and scarce resources. Pro se's with obviously frivolous cases will also not be—because they can't be—helped.

The Mission of My Company: A Statement

Company members working on intake should endeavor to ensure that they have the following information from or about individuals writing to or calling members of my company (often Posner himself) for help:

1. Sentence(s) and offense(s) for which they are currently serving their term.
2. Any and all appeals they have filed in the past and their outcomes.
3. Any information related to ongoing litigation (they may explain in a letter why they believe they have a strong case. They should enclose copies of any transcripts, case documents, affidavits, etc. that are related to the case).
4. A list of any lawyers or legal aid organizations that they have contacted about the case and the responses they received.

My company will decide which cases have sufficient merit to assign to pro bono lawyers or to non-lawyers. I will contact those individuals whose cases are not accepted by my company, giving the reasons why their case was not accepted. I may also refer those individuals to other legal aid providers in their area who may be able to help them. Once the company's intake staff has selected the most meritorious cases and recommended a few lawyers in the state that are qualified to take on the case, I will assign it to the best pro bono lawyer (or a non-lawyer, should the case not involve many legal technicalities). The lawyers may count hours spent on cases they handle for my company toward their state bar's pro bono hours requirements. Nonlawyer company members who have extensive experience litigating on behalf of themselves as pro se's will assist pro se's who do not require extensive guidance to handle their cases themselves. At present these company members include Brian Vukadinovich, Patrick Thesing, Edward Blum, Kenneth Abraham, and Shana Pollak. I will endeavor to produce guidance materials to help litigants represent themselves, along with other training materials including a certification program to train prisoners for job placement as paralegals.

I will assign meritorious cases to the lawyers able to practice in the relevant court. Pro bono lawyers will be expected to take on at least one pro se case a year to maintain their affiliation with my company. Mindful however of the limited resources and time that lawyers can devote to particular cases, my company will notify pro se's that their lawyer may need to negotiate fees with them if their case is particularly complicated or time-consuming. These discussions will be left up to the pro se turned client and his lawyer.

Lawyers working with my company should maintain their own malpractice insurance. They should also notify their firm of their involvement in my company's cases, should there be any conflicts of interest. I will track the workloads of the lawyers and non-lawyers to ensure that no volunteer takes on too much work. I will also correspond directly with those pro se's whose cases are not sufficiently meritorious to be accepted by my company; I will refer those individuals to other legal aid providers. I will also liaise with other legal service providers and donors. And don't forget that I run Justice for Pro Se's without accepting any monetary compensation.

Can My Company Become Involved in Class Actions?

I intended to end this book by reminding every member of my company of the importance of their reporting to me (whether directly or through the "callers" whom I mentioned earlier) from time to time the activities they have undertaken on behalf of pro se's. *Only by such reporting can I evaluate the progress of the company.* It's an important reminder, but shortly after formulating it I unexpectedly received an equally important reminder, from Pamela McKinney, that I consider the possibility of sometimes and perhaps often bringing class actions on behalf of pro se prison inmates, rather than just individual actions. The letters and phone calls in which pro se inmates request help from my company tend to focus very narrowly, and often confusingly, on the very specific individual characteristics of the inmate's case, which tend to be idiosyncratic and difficult to work into a lucid courtroom submission. In a class action suit in contrast to an individual suit, the members of the class have by definition of a class action common aims and concerns. The case they present is almost certain to be more uniform, less idiosyncratic, therefore easier for the court to understand and evaluate, than an individual's case—and at least somewhat more likely than an individual's case to evoke a favorable outcome from the court. I therefore encourage the members of my company, in dealing with claims by pro se prison inmates, at least to explore the feasibility and possible success of aggregating claims into a class action on behalf of the inmates constituting a class with uniform characteristics.

Of Finance and Organization

A Note on the Company's Finances

I regret having to report that my company's finances are at present, and indeed have been since the company's beginning several months ago, parlous. In fact, the company has no money. What has enabled it nevertheless to function is that as explained earlier in the book I don't require the members of the company to work for the company full time. Many are members of law firms or are otherwise active fee-paid lawyers, and the income they derive may satisfy their financial needs, enabling them to take on pro se cases pro bono—that is, for nothing—as members of my company. But that is a balance that can change at any time, and my particular concern is that some or many members of my company will resign sooner or late in order to increase their income from clients who can pay for a lawyer's services. Earlier in the book, I presented a long list (List 3 I call it) of fine lawyers spread throughout the country, and I would like to enlist many or even most or all of them to join my company. My efforts have paid a few dividends, but as yet only a few.

To thrive, my company needs donations that it can use to provide compensation to its members and thereby solve the problem discussed in the preceding paragraph. My efforts to obtain donations have been strenuous, and include requests sent to almost a hundred lawyers in Chicago, but have thus far yielded only a few fruits (none in the case of my requests to those lawyers!)—not nearly enough to meet the company's needs.

I will keep trying. A natural source of donations to a new company is the company's board of directors. Earlier in this book I listed a dozen very impressive, very highly qualified, prospects for my board whom I invited to join and who I expected would if they joined make generous donations. But several have not responded to my invitation to join the board and none has yet made a donation to my company, with the non-negligible exception of Andrew Rosenfield's gift of the luxurious office suite on the 50th floor of 227 West Monroe Street in Chicago. However, as mentioned earlier in this book, Selvyn Seidel, whom I have persuaded to be the chairman of the board, has embarked on a program of trying to persuade the other designated members of the board to make generous donations to Justice for Pro Se's, and he undoubtedly will be one of the major donors himself.

Organizational Wind Up

Much more needs to be said about my company, but from here on I'll try to be brief:

Reporting. It is imperative that all members of Justice for Pro Se's report to me at the end of each month, either directly or via a Regional Director or Mr. Vukadinovich, what if anything he or she has done that month to strengthen the firm (as by making donations or otherwise enlarging the firm's budget, identifying potential donors, improving regional direction, performing other administrative duties, or—and this is especially important—recruiting for the firm primarily from List 3 lawyers or nonlawyer legal advisors), and—not least—what if anything he or she has done to assist pro se's. It is essential that everything done for the firm constitute assistance to pro se's, for pro se's are the charitable object of the firm, and the Internal Revenue Service frequently audits ostensibly charitable enterprises to determine whether they are adhering to their stated charitable objectives. As noted very early in this book, Brian Vukadinovich and I will be sharing the important duty of overseeing the company's staff to assure proper reporting by them.

Compensating. By way of a quid pro quo, I or my successor or successors will every month compensate out of the firm's budget any member of the firm whose end-of-month report contributed net value to the company and/or to pro se's.

The Indigency Issue. Bruce R. Hopkins, the influential student of IRS audits whom I mentioned earlier, told me in a recent email that I must trim the scope of individuals who will be served by my organization to those litigants who, as a matter of law, are members of a charitable class; those he calls "the indigents." The implication is that only a poor person can be an object of charity. I disagree. I ask the reader to imagine a person who is neither wealthy nor poor but finds himself in some kind of legal trouble. Maybe he just lost his house to foreclosure—he thinks unjustly—but he has no idea of what to do. He has never been in litigation before; he has never hired a lawyer. He doesn't know what lawyers cost or what they do, specifically lawyers who handle foreclosure cases. He hears of a company called Justice for Pro Se's which provides legal assistance without charge to pro se's, defined as persons who do not have and cannot readily obtain representation by a lawyer. It appears to be Bruce Hopkins' position that because this person is not indigent, it is illegal for my company to provide him with free legal assistance. That would be a terrible result, and if I have to go to bat against the Internal Revenue Service to defeat what Mr. Hopkins says is its insistence that only indigents can be recipients of charitable legal assistance, I shall do so and I shall win.

Early on the evening of February 20 of this year (2018), I received a puzzling, and rather disconcerting, message from Hopkins, saying that my company—Justice for Pro Se's—should not provide legal assistance to pro se's unless they are either poor or "distressed" (undefined); to illustrate who should not receive legal assistance from my company, he gave the example of a billionaire pro se who asks me to provide him with a lawyer! I replied that I would not permit my company to provide lawyers for billionaires! To which I now add: no wealthy person has asked my company to provide him or her with a lawyer.

Professor David Zarfes of the University of Chicago Law School, who together with his brilliant students Brian Crush and Philip Acevedo had made important—indeed essential—contributions to the formation and structure of my company, responded to Hopkins and copied me on the response, which I now quote almost in full, though I have made a few minor editorial changes:

"Judge Posner attempted to respond to your earlier e-mail regarding the classification of individuals entitled to receive legal assistance from his pro se organization, but as the reply address he had for you was not working, he asked that I share with you his thoughts.

"At the outset: he does not intend to provide legal assistance to well-heeled individuals. His assumption is that such individuals will not be seeking legal assistance from a pro se organization. He therefore plans to provide a lawyer or other legal assistance (including training the pro se to be his own courtroom lawyer, which is often more effective than giving him a lawyer) not to the rich but to a nonwealthy pro se whose legal claim has at least some potential merit.

"Judge Posner has no clear idea of what a non-poor pro se who is 'distressed' is like, but he knows that many pro se's are upset about their situation to the extent of needing assistance even if they are not poor, and he wonders if perhaps 'upset' is a suitable synonym for distressed in the pro se context. Might such an adjective be used to address the classification—for example, 'Unrepresented [or "Pro se"] litigants facing potential upset in court proceedings'?

"One question I have [this is still Professor Zarfes's comment on the Hopkins missive] is how a nonprofit organization like the ACLU has been able (to my mind) to circumvent the classification issue. To my knowledge, they select cases and clients based upon the importance of the issue to the organization. I'm not sure they apply a means test to their litigants. For what it's worth, the ACLU's stated mission is "to defend and preserve the individual rights and liberties guaranteed to every person in this country by the Constitution and laws of the United States," though 'every person' strikes me as terribly broad." Professor Zarfes added: "Drawing upon the ACLU approach, perhaps we should focus on something along the lines of "serving the ends of justice"/"providing improved access to the courts"/"leveling the playing field..."] by offering legal assistance to pro se litigants."

My [i.e. Posner's] initial response was that it was too late to counter Hopkins' plainly deficient argument, because the draft of my book had been sent to Amazon CreateSpace the day before the exchanges I've been quoting, and with characteristic speed Amazon had already confirmed the receipt of the draft and its decision to publish it and I had agreed on the terms of payment! But I was wrong. I had ordered only 100 copies of the book from Amazon. Although those could not be changed, they were just for members of my company. I would soon be ordering at least 200 more copies—copies that could—and in light of the discussion in this email would—be revised to include Professor Zarfes' response to Hopkins. As explained by George Rumsey, the technical genius (I do not exaggerate) who provides the final edits to my books, "it is too late to change the copies we already ordered, since they're in process of being printed. But we can definitely change the book itself for future use, with no problem. We just need to decide where to put the pertinent information. Since those 100 copies are for 'private' corporate use, there shouldn't be a problem."

The 100 copies were distributed to the members of the company. I was planning to order 200 more from Amazon, but was stopped by the realization, explained on page 2 of the present book, that the book, the 100 copies I'd obtained and 200 more that I'd planned to obtain, required a number of corrections—the corrections made in this redraft of the book.

I and the other members of my company will decide which cases have sufficient merit to be assigned to pro bono lawyers or to non-lawyers. I'll contact those individuals whose cases are rejected, giving the reasons for the rejection, and I may also refer those individuals to other providers of legal assistance who may be able to help them.

I was gratified to come across recently a list of leading Chicago law firms that provide assistance to persons who have legal claims or issues but lack legal sophistication and therefore depend on the generosity of such firms:

1. Sidley and Austin's "Capital Litigation Project" (for Alabama Prisoners on Death Row).
2. Northwestern's MacArthur Justice Center (for indigent prisoners in Chicago).
3. Cabrini Green Legal Aid (for litigants with criminal and civil cases).
4. Legal Assistance Foundation (for undocumented immigrants, indigent tenants, indigent families).
5. Uptown People's Law Center (for Illinois prisoners).

Notice that only one of the five—number 2, the well-known MacArthur Justice Center—appears to cater exclusively to indigents. And it turns out that the appearance of exclusivity is false. For if you google MacArthur Justice Center, you'll discover that it has at least as broad a scope as any of the other four.

I should point out moreover that the five firms listed above are but a small fraction of the number of firms that provide aid to persons who have legal claims but cannot muster the assets necessary to hire a lawyer. See, for broader lists of such firms, my book *Improving the Federal Judiciary: Staff Attorney Programs, the Plight of the Pro Se's, and the Televising of Oral Arguments* 95-96, 103-08 (Dec. 4, 2017); and Chicago Bar Foundation, "Pro Bono Volunteer Opportunities for Attorneys in the Chicago Area" (n.d.).

The Future

My company is young, its future promising. I see it expanding geographically to encompass the entire nation, including its non-state off-shore possessions; I see its personnel growing, and its relations to law firms and lawyers and pro se's in its territories intensifying. I see it obtaining a far-deeper understanding of the pro se phenomenon, the pro se culture. (As noted in a U.S. Courts Bulletin, *Pro Se Centers Help Even the Odds for Litigants Without Lawyers*, Aug. 20, 2015, at http://www.uscourts.gov/news/2015/08/20/pro-se-centers-help-even-odds-litigants-without-lawyers. This is certainly the outlook of my company.)

I see the Regional Directors building the firm in their regions. I see the board of directors pushing the company in constructive directions, as well as enriching it through donations provided by or solicited by the directors. I see, in short, a bright future.

Richard A. Posner

CODA:
How Team Posner Inc. Molted into Justice for Pro Se's and Then into Posner Center of Justice for Pro Se's

An outstanding client of mine, Ted Martin by name, by sports fans known as the world champion of Hacky Sack, advised me to change the name of my company from Team Posner Inc. to The Justice League, and I thought it over, and finally agreed, because I don't think my name should be in the title, because I think "Team" is a silly word for a company, and because "Justice" conveys a much better sense of what I'm trying to do: obtain justice for pro se's. But my chief research assistant, Theresa Yuan, discovered that there are several pro bono firms with names so similar to the Justice League as to invite possible trademark suits, so I modified Mr. Martin's suggestion by changing the name of my company to Justice for Pro Se's.

And so ends the analytical body of this book. What follows and completes it is an appendix with several components including an index.

Web Preview

Justice for Pro Se's will have a website communication from and with the company. The website, www.justice-for-pro-ses.org, is not yet on-line but a Webview Preview has been created—this is that preview.

OUR MISSION STATEMENT

Justice for Pro Se's is a nationwide *pro bono* legal-services organization founded and led by Richard A. Posner, a retired judge on the U.S. Court of Appeals for the Seventh Circuit. **Justice for Pro Se's** was founded on the belief that pro se litigants are being mistreated by the courts because judges are often indifferent or hostile to them.

Justice for Pro Se's is not a law firm. Instead, it is a 501(c)(3) organization devoted to assisting deserving pro se litigants who need, but cannot afford or don't know how to utilize, legal assistance or guidance. **Justice for Pro Se's** includes lawyers among its members, but they are in the nature of volunteer helpers; they are not employees.

Justice for Pro Se's refers deserving pro se litigants to outside lawyers and others willing to assist the litigants free of charge in representing themselves in state or federal court. **Justice for Pro Se's** will then monitor the pro se's cases, publish the results, and thereby bring accountability to the courts.

RICHARD A. POSNER
(Our Founder)

Richard Allen Posner was a Judge of the United States Court of Appeals for the Seventh Circuit in Chicago from 1981 until 2017.

Judge Posner is currently a Senior Lecturer at the University of Chicago Law School. His faculty profile can be found at: https://www.law.uchicago.edu/faculty/posner-r.

Judge Posner has been described as "probably America's greatest living jurist" (*Wikipedia*). A 2004 poll by *Legal Affairs* magazine named him as one of the top twenty legal thinkers in the United States. In addition, a 2000 study published in *The Journal of Legal Studies* identified Judge Posner as the most-cited legal scholar of all time. He is the author of 68 books and countless scholarly articles.

As the sole owner of Justice for Pro Se's, Judge Posner has committed not to receive a single penny from the company whether as compensation, pay back, incentive pay, reward, or otherwise characterized.

Wikimedia Commons
(chensiyuan - chensiyuan)

Shutterstock.com

ABOUT

After 35 years, Judge Richard A. Posner resigned from the United States Court of Appeals for the Seventh Circuit because he believed that pro se litigants were not getting a fair shake from either his court or any other court. So he decided to quit and do something to change that. Here is why:

As Judge Posner wrote in his dissent in *Estate of Miller v. Marberry*, 847 F.3d 425, 429-433 (7th Cir. 2017), the Court of Appeals panel's majority decision was "unconscionable" because it allowed a prison to knowingly violate its clear legal duties in such a way as to seriously injure an inmate and thereby hasten his death. As Judge Posner added: "A dog would have deserved better treatment."

As a result, the panel majority let stand the district court's erroneous grant of summary judgment to the prison, which not only denied the inmate's claim, but also took away the inmate's constitutional right to have a jury – not a judge – decide that claim.

Judge Posner also called the appellate panel majority's decision "outrageous" because, like the decision of the district court, it was based on a clear misstatement of the facts. Moreover, even after the factual misstatements were privately acknowledged, a majority of the entire Court of Appeals voted to deny a rehearing of the case on the specious grounds that the errors were those of fact, not law.

Apparently, some judges believe that factual errors in a judicial decision need not be corrected because they are hidden, whereas legal errors are not. Yet, an accurate statement of the facts would have mandated that the inmate be allowed to present his case to a jury, which would have then undoubtedly ruled in the inmate's favor, as discussed in the excerpt below from one of Judge Posner's recent books.

The following excerpt is reprinted with permission from:

*Reforming the Federal Judiciary: My Former Court
Needs to Overhaul Its Staff Attorney Program
and Begin Televising Its Oral Arguments*
by Richard A. Posner, pp. 23-27

The decision in *Estate of Miller* [*v. Marberry*, 847 F.3d 425 (7th Cir. 2017), *rehearing denied, rehearing en banc denied*] was in my view particularly unfortunate. Miller's first stop upon his arrival at the prison was at the prison's medical clinic, where either he informed the medical staff or the staff informed him that he had a brain tumor, and the staff told him that his tumor was interfering with his balance and therefore he had to be given the lower bunk in whatever cell he was assigned to, as his tumor might cause him to fall and possibly injure himself very seriously if he was climbing up to or down from the upper bunk in his cell. He so advised the guard in the cellblock to which he was assigned, but the guard assigned him to an upper bunk because Miller could not produce a document specifying his lower-bunk assignment. ("Where's your document?" the guard asked him without explaining what document he was referring to.) The guard refused to check with the clinic, which had the record of Miller's lower-bunk assignment. As for Miller, he seems not to have known what the guard meant by the question "Where's your document?"

Sure enough, assigned to the upper bunk, Miller soon fell, was seriously injured, and had to be hospitalized. Returned to the prison, he was again assigned to an upper bunk and again fell and again was seriously injured. He complained repeatedly to the prison's warden about not being assigned to a lower bunk (for she frequently walked through the cellblocks and often walked right past Miller's cell and he would remind her of his need for an upper bunk, but she said nothing in response and did nothing).

After his return to prison following his second fall, Miller sued Rogers [the guard] and Marberry [the warden] for deliberate indifference to a serious medical problem, in violation of his Eighth Amendment rights. But he died during the litigation, and while the suit was continued by his family, eventually the district court granted summary judgment in favor of the two defendants.

Miller's treatment by both guard and warden was unconscionable, as was [Seventh Circuit Court of Appeals] Judge Easterbrook's and Judge Sykes's decision upholding the district court's unjustifiable ruling in favor of the guard and the warden.

Here is a shortened version of my dissent. ... [A]s this court said in *Dobbey v. Mitchell-Lawshea*, 806 F.3d 938, 941 (7th Cir. 2015) – an opinion of mine – "prison guards have a responsibility for prisoners' welfare. If a prisoner is writhing in agony, the guard cannot ignore him on the grounds of not being a doctor; he has to make an effort to find a doctor, or in this case a dentist or a technician, or a pharmacist – some medical professional." See also *Smego v. Mitchell*, 723 F.3d 752, 757 (7th Cir. 2013). If that's true of a mere guard, it is *a fortiori* true of a warden who knows that a prisoner's potentially very dangerous health condition is being ignored by the prison's guards, whom she – the warden – supervises.

Miller was a federal prison inmate, and the Federal Bureau of Prisons, be it noted, is required by law to "provide suitable quarters and provide for the safekeeping, care, and subsistence of all persons charged with or convicted of offenses against the United States. . . ." 18 U.S.C. § 4042(a)(2). The Bureau failed. Quarters with an upper-bunk assignment are not suitable for someone with the kind of brain tumor that Miller had; he was denied both safekeeping and care. This is a classic case of turning a blind eye "to a substantial risk of serious harm to a prisoner." *Perez v. Fenoglio*, 792 F.3d 768, 781 (7th Cir. 2015). That is what is called "deliberate indifference" – a serious constitutional offense.

I consider the decision outrageous, but for completeness wish to mention briefly Judge Easterbrook's response to a subsequent motion by me (joined by Judges Kanne and Hamilton, but voted down by the court) to rehear the case en banc. He remarks that . . . . "[t]he panel majority [that is, Judges Easterbrook and Sykes] resolved the case by observing that Miller had not sued persons responsible for issuing or implementing bunk passes." Now this is a strange statement – for why on earth would Miller have sued persons who had issued a lower-bunk pass for him. . . .

Judge Easterbrook says I contended in my dissent that Rogers and/or Marberry "should have helped [Miller] out, even though doing so was not part of their duties." Not part of their duties? Preventing serious injury to an inmate is not a duty of prison staff even when they can perform the duty without cost or risk? All Rogers or Marberry had to do was find an empty lower bunk for Miller, and we know there were empty lower bunks in the prison; the prison wasn't full up.

The decision by my colleagues was heartless; I imagine they're puzzled that I care.

A Postscript to *Estate of Miller v. Marberry*

The same disastrous result in *Estate of Miller* almost occurred one month earlier in the case of *Glisson v. Indiana Dept. of Corrections*, 849 F.3d 372 (7th Cir. 2017). In *Glisson* (which was not a pro se case), the prison inmate was literally starved to death. Once again, the district court dismissed the inmate's clearly-meritorious claim before that claim could be presented to a jury, and the Court of Appeals panel's majority then affirmed that erroneous dismissal.

Also, once again, both the district court and the appellate panel's majority in *Glisson* justified their adverse decisions by misstating the facts. However, the full Court of Appeals later reheard the case, corrected the factual misstatements, and properly found in favor of the inmate.

OUR COURT CASES

Prisoner Pro Se Cases

- PRISONER ABUSE CASES
- WAR ON DRUGS CASES
- HABEAS CORPUS CASES
- POLICE BRUTALITY CASES
- SENTENCING CASES
- CRIMINAL PROSECUTION CASES

Other Pro Se Cases

- CIVIL RIGHTS CASES
- TORTS CASES
- EQUITABLE CLAIMS CASES
- EMPLOYMENT DISCRIMINATION CASES
- CONTRACTS CASES
- LEGAL MALPRACTICE CASES

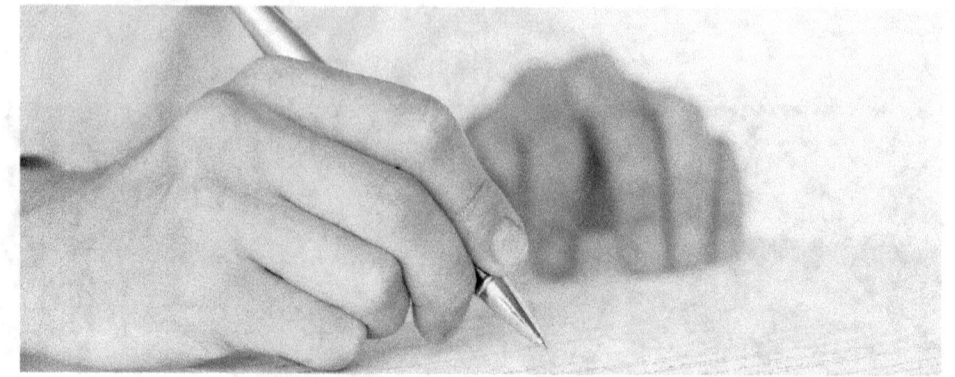

INTAKE FORMS
GENERAL INFORMATION

Justice for Pro Se's is not a law firm and it does not have or represent clients. Also, while **Justice for Pro Se's** does include lawyers among its members, they are in the nature of volunteer helpers -- not employees.

Instead, **Justice for Pro Se's** is a non-profit legal-referral service for deserving pro se litigants who need (but cannot afford or don't know how to utilize) legal assistance or guidance. We are developing an extensive list of both lawyers and non-lawyers throughout the United States who have indicated a willingness to assist pro se litigants free of charge. To request such assistance, please fill out the *Intake Form* below.

If the person to whom we refer you decides to assist you, that person will advise you on what you will need to do to handle the case by yourself in court. For example, this person might agree to guide your legal filings, provide some case law support, suggest legal arguments for you to make, direct your litigation tactics and strategy, or prepare you for your trial or appellate oral argument.

If the judge in your case allows it, this person might also assist you in preparing your legal pleadings and court briefs. However, if this person prepares any documents for you, through those documents that person will typically identify him or herself and describe the limited role that he or she is playing in your litigation.

In very rare instances, this person might also make a court appearance on your behalf. But, in general, you will be handling all in-court work (court hearings, the trial, and the appellate oral argument) by yourself.

Thus, to repeat, the person to whom we refer you will not be representing you in court. If you want to have someone represent you in court, you must go to a legal-aid office or hire a private lawyer.

A FORM FOR ALL PRO SE LITIGANTS TO FILL OUT

If you have a pro se case and you would like us to try to find someone who might be willing to assist you in representing yourself, please fill out the form below. Also, please note that there is a second form for prison inmates to complete.

Name

Phone

Email

Address

City

State
Select ▼

Zip Code

Are you requesting a lawyer to represent you and take over all aspects of your case? Yes No

Are you merely requesting a referral to someone who can give you assistance so that you can represent yourself? Yes No

State the type of case (such as criminal or civil) and the issues involved. Please be specific:

Has the case been filed in court yet? Yes No

If the case has been filed in court, please provide the title of the case, the court in which it was filed, the case number, the name of the judge, the location of the court, and the name of the opposing lawyer(s):

If the case has been filed in court, please explain the status of the case (what has already happened in your court case and what still needs to happen in the future):

If you are currently being represented by a lawyer in this case, please provide the lawyer's name and contact information:

If you have previously been represented by a lawyer in this case (but you are not now being represented by a lawyer), please provide the previous lawyer's name, the lawyer's contact information, and the reason that this lawyer is no longer representing you:

If you have any evidence to support your claims, please describe that evidence:

Submit

Information sent through this "Intake Form" form or by email is not necessarily secure. Please do not transmit confidential information. Email sent to Justice for Pro Se's or any of its members or affiliates will not establish an attorney-client relationship. The information you obtain on our website is not, nor is it intended to be, legal advice, nor is it intended to create an attorney-client relationship. Please read our Disclaimer for more information.

A FORM FOR PRISON INMATES TO FILL OUT

If you are a prison inmate with a pro se case, please complete the form below in addition to the previous form.

Name Phone Email

Address City State Zip Code

Please list the sentence(s) and offense(s) for which you are currently serving your term:

Please describe any and all appeals that you have filed in the past and their outcomes:

Please describe any ongoing litigation in which you are currently involved:

Please explain why you think that you have a strong case:

Please list all lawyers or legal-aid organizations that you have contacted about your case and explain the responses that you have received:

Submit

Information sent through this "Intake Form" form or by email is not necessarily secure. Please do not transmit confidential information. Email sent to Justice for Pro Se's or any of its members or affiliates will not establish an attorney-client relationship. The information you obtain on our website is not, nor is it intended to be, legal advice, nor is it intended to create an attorney-client relationship. Please read our Disclaimer for more information.

RESOURCES FOR PRO SE LITIGANTS

Below are a number of self-help publications for pro se litigants.

- Guide for Pro Se Civil Litigants
- Guide to Filing a Prisoner Suit
- Pro Se Tips #1 (Civil)
- Pro Se Tips #1 (Prisoner Cases)
- Pro Se Tips #2 (Civil)
- Pro Se Tips #2 (Prisoner Cases)
- Pro Se Tips #3 (Civil)
- Pro Se Tips #3 (Prisoner Cases)
- Pro Se Litigation Forms
- Court Rules

Shutterstock.com

DONATE

Make a Tax-Deductible Gift to Justice for Pro Se's

Select an amount:

$300 $500 $1000 $5000   Other

DONATE NOW

Appendix
Judge Gilman's Writing Rules: Heed Them: Staff Attorneys, Law Clerks, Judges[1]

As should be apparent from the discussion in this book, the members of Justice for Pro Se's are going to be involved in a lot of writing—writing to pro se's, writing to judges and lawyers, writing to me, writing to each other. Writing does not come easily to most Americans, including most judges and lawyers, most clients, and most seekers of legal help, including of course pro se's. This outstanding catalog of writing rules—the product of senior judge Ronald Lee Gilman of the court of appeals for the Sixth Circuit—should be must reading for all readers of this book, as well as all member of Justice for Pro Se's.

---

[1] "Effective Brief Writing," in U.S. Court of Appeals Judge Ronald Lee Gilman, "How to Magically Win on Appeal," Federal Bar Association Seminar, Oct. 28, 2016, www.fedbar.org/Image-Library/Memphis-Mid-South-Chapter/Judge-Gilman--How-to-Magically-Win-on-Appeal.aspx?FT=.pdf.

A. General Principles

1. ***Consistency.*** Be consistent with use of words and phrases.
2. ***Footnotes.*** No footnotes. Ever.
3. ***Legal lingo.*** Avoid legal lingo. (Bad: "He was convicted on two felony firearm counts." Good: "He was convicted on two counts of being a felon in possession of a firearm.")
4. ***Respect.*** Be respectful of the parties and other judges. Do not engage in personal attacks or use disparaging language. Criticism is more effective when it is not cloaked in hyperbole.
5. ***Wordiness.*** Be concise, not verbose.

B. Sentence Structure

1. ***Adverbs.*** Place adverbs before verbs. (Bad: "He assumes erroneously that the list is exhaustive." Good: "He erroneously assumes that the list is exhaustive.")
2. ***Capitalization.*** Capitalize the titles of specific documents, but not the generic names of documents. You should capitalize "court" only when referring to the United States Supreme Court or the full name of a court.
3. ***Colons.*** Two spaces should follow a colon. The first letter following a colon should be lowercase unless the phrase following the colon is a complete sentence.
4. ***Commas.*** Generally, insert a comma before the conjunction "but" when it is used in a sentence. But a comma is not necessary in a short sentence. (Example: "The government's argument is sensible but ultimately unpersuasive.") Also insert a comma before "which" when it is used within a sentence as a relative pronoun.

5. ***Double negatives.*** Avoid sentences with double negatives. (Bad: "This does not mean that he is not disabled." Good: "This does not preclude a finding that he is disabled.")

6. ***Em dashes.*** You may use an em dash in a sentence to indicate a parenthetical thought. Place an em dash by inserting three hyphens.

7. ***First and last words.*** No two consecutive sentences should begin or end with the same word.

8. ***Hard spaces/hyphens.*** As a general rule, Judge G does not like hyphens, numbers, or symbols dangling at the end of a line. Specifically, you will need to place a hard space (by holding down the control button while you strike the space bar) between numbers in an *enumerated series* and the word immediately following the number. For example, if your sentence included a list of factors such as "(1) seriousness of the offense, (2) characteristics of the defendant," you would need to insert one hard space between "(1)" and "seriousness," and a second hard space between "(2)" and "characteristics." You also need to insert a hard space between a *record citation* and the cited page or document number. For instance, if you cite "DE 32 at 5," insert a hard space between "DE" and "32." Similarly, if you cite "JA 289," insert a hard space between "JA" and "289." Place a hard space between *symbols* (such as § or ¶) and their corresponding numbers ("§ 1983"). In addition, insert hard spaces between the periods in an ellipsis to avoid breaking the *ellipsis* over two lines. In Word, a hard space can be created using ctrl + shift + spacebar (i.e., hitting the spacebar while holding the control and shift keys down). The shortcut in WordPerfect is ctrl + spacebar. Finally, place a hard hyphen between *number ranges* ("7-10"). In Word, the shortcut is ctrl + shift + -. The WordPerfect shortcut is ctrl + -.

9. ***Headings.*** Capitalize only the first word in a heading or subheading.

10. ***Identifying the lower court.*** When you first describe a lower court in a paragraph, identify the specific court ("bankruptcy court," "district court"). You should then use "the court" throughout the remainder of the paragraph, unless either you mention another court within the same paragraph or use of "the court" would otherwise be confusing.

11. ***Introductory clausitis.*** Do not begin more than two consecutive sentences with an introductory clause.

12. ***Length.*** Shorter sentences are better than longer sentences. Vary the length of sentences.

13. ***Lists.*** Use serial commas in a list of three or more items. (Example: "Despite his disability, Smith could walk, run, and swim.") Do not use semicolons, unless one or more of the individual list items contain commas (semicolons are okay in other contexts, of course).

14. ***Passive voice.*** Feel free to occasionally use the passive voice, especially if the meaning is clear and an awkward present-tense phrasing would otherwise result.

15. ***Possessives.*** Avoid using two or more possessives in a row (for example, do not use "Smith's mother's house").

16. ***Sentence spacing.*** Two spaces should follow the period at the end of each sentence.

17. ***Split infinitives.*** If splitting an infinitive sounds more natural, then split it.

18. ***Transitions.*** Do not begin sentences with "however" or "therefore." (Put these terms in the body of the sentence instead.) Sentences may, however, begin with "And," "But," and "Moreover."

19. Verb Tense. Be careful to use the correct verb tense. This problem comes up most often with the present tense: you should use the present tense where a fact is still true or where the described thing is still in existence.

C. Word Use

1. Preferred and Disfavored Words

Approximately. Use "approximately" instead of "about." (Example: "The package weighed approximately four grams.") "About" means "regarding" and should be used accordingly.

Attorney fees. Use the phrase "attorney fees," not "attorney's fees," "attorneys' fees," or "attorneys fees."

Because. Do not use "as" as a substitute for "because."

Court/judge. Describe the actions of the lower court ("the district court") rather than the judge ("the district judge"), unless context requires you to refer to the judge individually.

Even though. Use "even though" instead of "despite the fact that."

Finally. Use "finally" instead of "lastly."

In addition. Use "in addition" instead of "additionally."

Pleaded. Use "pleaded" rather than "pled."

Present case. As a general rule, use "in the present case" instead of "here." But use both phrases where one would otherwise appear numerous times in a confined space.

Record. Use "in the record" rather than "on the record."

Regarding. Use "regarding" or "concerning" instead of "as to."

Stated. Stated is a fairly nondescript word. If possible, use another word, such as "reasoned," "concluded," "explained," etc.

Words to avoid. Avoid the words "merely" and "some." Use "clearly" and "thus" sparingly.

2. **Word Usage**

Abbreviations. Do not put quotation marks around abbreviations, i.e., (ERISA), not ("ERISA").

Caselaw. Judge Gilman prefers to use "caselaw" as one word, not two.

Compound adjectives. Hyphenate most compound adjectives ("independent-source doctrine," "ineffective-assistance-of-counsel claim," "narcotics-detection dog"). But do not hyphenate an adverb ending in -ly. ("properly pled complaint," "particularly described property"). And do not hyphenate compound adjectives that are used most commonly without hyphenation ("district court ruling," "due process clause," "good faith effort," or "summary judgment order").

Court identifiers. Use "this court" when referring to prior decisions of the Sixth Circuit; use "we" when referring to the present case. Never use "we" in a bench memorandum. The "Supreme Court" means the U.S. Supreme Court. References to the supreme court of a state should include the name of that state (e.g., "the Michigan Supreme Court").

Criminal convictions. A defendant is convicted *on* a particular count ("Smith was convicted on count four of the indictment"), but is convicted *of* a specific crime ("Smith was convicted of conspiracy to possess and distribute cocaine").

Dates. Use "October 1998" and not "October, 1998" or even "October of 1998." Also, do not as a matter of course include a comma after a full date, unless the comma would otherwise be appropriate in the sentence. (*For example:* "Unlike the evening of August 30, 2005, the evening of August 31, 2005 was hot and rainy.")

Describing certain court actions. Courts make factual *findings* and reach legal *conclusions*. *Holdings* are dispositive rulings.

Distinctions. Observe the distinctions between the following terms:

that (defining/restrictive)	*which* (nondefining/nonrestrictive)
where (place)	*when* (temporal)
because (causal)	*since* (temporal)
although (contrast)	*while* (temporal)
may (permissive)	*might* (potential)

English words. Use English words whenever possible. (Bad: "Smith alleged, inter alia, that Jones had violated her constitutional rights." Good: "Smith alleged, among other things, that Jones had violated her constitutional rights.")

It. Do not use "it" as an indefinite pronoun. (Bad: "It goes without saying that Bob is a generous man.")

Last names. When referring to parties with the same last name — for instance, Elvis Presley and Priscilla Presley — you can use "the Presleys" to refer to the group, and "Elvis" and "Priscilla" to refer to the individuals.

Latin words and phrases. Common Latin words are not italicized, such as habeas corpus, de novo, sua sponte, etc. Never use the Latin words "supra" or "infra." Use "above" or "below" instead. Uncommon Latin words and phrases, such as *in abstentia*, should be italicized.

Names ending in "s." An individual whose last name ends in "s" takes the possessive form of apostrophe plus "s." But the plural possessive is indicated by only an apostrophe. (*Example*: "John Woods's dog is named Spot." On the other hand, "The Bonds' family dog is named Sandy.")

Numbers. Spell out numbers less than 10, unless there are higher numbers in the same sentence that the lower numbers are being compared to.

Only. Be sure that "only" is modifying the correct word. (Bad: "Relief is only available if both conditions are met." Good: "Relief is available only if both conditions are met." Bad: "The package only contained cocaine." Good: "The package contained only cocaine.")

Party names. Avoid formalistic names for the parties. (Use "Jones" instead of "Plaintiff-Appellant.")

Prefixes. Avoid hyphenating prefixes, unless a visual monstrosity results. ("Postconviction" is fine. "Prepresidential" is not.)

Series. Names or concepts in a series or list should appear in alphabetical order, unless another organizing principle would make more sense given the context.

Standard of review. When explaining the standard of review that the court applies, do not say that the court "reviews for clear error" or "reviews for abuse of discretion." Judge G instead prefers that you say that this court reviews the district court's judgment "under the clear-error standard" or the "abuse-of-discretion standard." In the case of de novo review, however, you may say that this court "reviews de novo a district court's grant of summary judgment."

That. Use the relative pronoun to avoid miscues. (Bad: "The government charged the lease deal sprang from a web of deceit." Good: "The government charged that the lease deal sprang from a web of deceit.") Do not, however, use more than two "that"s in a row in a sentence. Rephrase or eliminate one of the relative pronouns to avoid this result.

D. Citation Style

1. *Alterations to quoted text.* When removing alterations from a quotation, such as brackets or an ellipsis, indicate the specific alterations omitted in a parenthetical. Also indicate if you remove any citations or quotation marks within the same parenthetical, and list all of these items in alphabetical order.

   A special note regarding omitted quotation marks. When omitting quotation marks, include the word "internal." In other words, your parenthetical would be "(internal quotation marks omitted)." Also, be careful not to use "quotations" instead of "quotation marks."

   Some examples.

   (brackets and ellipsis omitted)

   (citation and internal quotation marks omitted)

   (brackets, citations, ellipses, footnotes, and internal quotation marks omitted)

2. *Citing and quoting parentheticals.* You should use a "citing" parenthetical only if the additional source is particularly relevant (for example, the source is a Supreme Court case, a bedrock Sixth Circuit case, or a case from a special-

ized court). Use a quoting parenthetical, however, if you are quoting language that is itself quoting another source.

Note that, per Bluebook Rule 5.3(c), "citation omitted" is appropriate where the citation is being left out of the quoted portion of text. A different situation arises, however, where the quoted language quotes another source, but the citation to this underlying source is *not* itself part of the language that you are quoting. In this situation, Bluebook Rule 5.2(e) recommends using a quoting parenthetical rather than omitting quotation marks and using "internal quotation marks omitted" and "citation omitted" parentheticals. In the 20th edition, Bluebook Rule 1.5(b) no longer recognizes the use of the "internal quotation marks omitted" parenthetical. Bluebook Rule 5.2(f) allows for the omission of internal quotation marks only when the opening mark appears at the beginning of the language that you are quoting and the closing mark appears at the end of the language.

For example, suppose you want to quote the following language from *International Dairy Foods Association v. Boggs*, 622 F.3d 628, 635 (6th Cir. 2010): "By contrast, the decision of whether to grant a motion for a preliminary injunction is 'left to the sound discretion of the district court.' *Deja Vu of Cincinnati, L.L.C. v. Union Twp. Bd. of Trs.*, 411 F.3d 777, 782 (6th Cir. 2005)." According to 5.2(e), you would cite it as follows: "By contrast, the decision of whether to grant a motion for a preliminary injunction is 'left to the sound discretion of the district court.'" *Int'l Dairy Foods Assoc. v. Boggs*, 622 F.3d 628, 635 (6th Cir. 2010) (quoting *Deja Vu of Cincinnati, L.L.C. v. Union Twp. Bd. of Trs.*, 411 F.3d 777, 782 (6th Cir. 2005)).

3. ***Emphasis added (when citing to something in the record).*** When the emphasis-added descriptor does not directly follow a citation, such as in an opinion where you have deleted the record citation for the quotation, treat it as an abridged

sentence and place it in parentheses, with the "e" capitalized. (*Example*: [big long block quote] (Emphasis added.)) Note that the period is placed inside of the parentheses.

4. *Emphasis in original.* In a rare break from the Blue Book, Judge G prefers that you indicate parenthetically if the emphasis in a quoted source is from the original text.

5. *Hard spaces.* Do not split section marks (§) and their section numbers across lines. To avoid this, insert a hard space. This rule also applies to not splitting JA citations from their page numbers, or docket entries from their entry number, or a list of numbers from their accompanying items. In Word, a hard space can be created using ctrl + shift + spacebar (i.e., hitting the spacebar while holding the control and shift keys down). The shortcut in WordPerfect is ctrl + spacebar.

6. *Other opinions, references to.* Cite as either "Maj. Op." (when dissenting or when concurring in part and dissenting in part), "Lead Op." (when concurring), or "Dissenting Op." (when writing the majority). *Example*: The majority also states that the Jehovah's Witnesses "may spread their message at stores, on street corners, in restaurants, in parks, and other public forums." (Maj. Op. at 21)

7. *Parenthetical explanations.* Include these as often as possible after a case citation unless they would be unnecessarily duplicative of the cited proposition or sentence. Remember not to omit articles such as "the," "a," and "an" from the parenthetical. Begin these parentheticals with a gerund, unless you are quoting a complete sentence.

8. *Parts, references to.* When referring to a portion of a memorandum or opinion, place periods after both the Roman numeral and the subpart letter or number. (*Example*: "As discussed above in Parts II.B. and III.A.2., this argument is without merit.") Use the word "Part" instead of the word "Section," and always capitalize "Part."

9. ***Pincites.*** Judge Gilman prefers that you not use pincites when summarizing the facts of an opinion unless you quote directly from the opinion. (*Example*: "The plaintiff in *Smith v. Jones* was a quadriplegic and blind in one eye." This does not require a citation to *Smith*. *But*: "She became a quadriplegic after a reckless driver 'sped through a stop light and collided with her vehicle'" would require a pincite to *Smith*.)

10. ***Record citations.*** Cite the record in parentheses. (*Example*: "When Burt provided a price acceptable to Holland, they shook hands and announced their agreement to the rest of the members at the meeting. (JA 934-35)") No periods should appear either inside or outside of the record citation. Remove citations to the record before submitting an opinion for filing.

11. ***Signals.*** When using the signal "*See, e.g.*," italicize everything except for the last comma.

12. ***Small caps.*** Do not use small caps. Use regular Roman type instead.

13. ***String cites.*** Use sparingly and, if used, include explanatory parentheticals.

14. ***Textual citations.*** When you refer to a case for the first time in a textual sentence, include the full case citation within that sentence.

15. ***Two-page rule.*** A source should be cited in full, even if previously cited in full, where that source has not been referred to in the prior two pages of text. The only exception is when the case cited is well known and repeatedly cited, such as *Miranda* or *Terry*.

16. ***Unpublished opinions.***

For opinions available via online databases only, follow this example: *Lyons v. TVA*, No. 87-5309, 1988 WL 12227, at *1 (6th Cir. Feb. 16, 1988).

For unpublished opinions available both in the Federal Appendix and online, cite to the Federal Appendix: *Lyons v. TVA*, 8 F. App'x 31 (6th Cir. 1998).

For opinions that have been designated for publication but have yet to be assigned to a federal reporter, follow this example: *Roberts v. Ward*, No. 05-6305, — F.3d —, 2006 WL 3392620, at * 2 (6th Cir. Nov. 27, 2006).

17. *U.S. Sentencing Guidelines.*

When used in text. The first time that you mention the federal sentencing guidelines, refer to them as the United States Sentencing Guidelines. After the first mention, you may thereafter refer to them as "the guidelines." You do not need to provide this shortened form in a parenthetical after the first reference.

When used in a citation. Follow Bluebook Rule 12.9.4 when citing to the guidelines, with the following considerations in mind. The text of a guideline is usually followed by commentary (abbreviated as "cmt.") The commentary includes all explanatory information that follows a guideline, and it often contains subsections for "Application Notes" and "Background" information. When citing to information that appears under the subheading of "Background," cite as U.S.S.G. § 2D1.2 cmt. background. Cite any numbered note in the commentary section—whether it appears under "Application Note" (*see, e.g.*, U.S.S.G. § 3D1.4) or not (*see, e.g.*, U.S.S.G. § 3D1.5)—as U.S.S.G. § [section number] cmt. n.1. And cite to a guidelines appendix as

U.S.S.G. app. C.

Exception: The Bluebook citation format refers to the guidelines as "U.S. Sentencing Guidelines Manual"—e.g.,.S. Sentencing Guidelines Manual § 3D1.1. When citing the guidelines in bench memos and opinions, you should instead use either "United States Sentencing Guidelines" (in the first reference to the guidelines, either in text or a citation) or "U.S.S.G." (if "United States Sentencing Guidelines" has already been referenced in either the text or an earlier citation).

Exception: Specify the guidelines version (i.e. 2010, 2015, etc.) only when relevant to the discussion.

E. General Principles

1. ***Consistency.*** Be consistent with use of words and phrases.
2. ***Footnotes.*** No footnotes. Ever.
3. ***Legal lingo.*** Avoid legal lingo. (Bad: "He was convicted on two felony firearm counts." Good: "He was convicted on two counts of being a felon in possession of a firearm.")
4. ***Respect.*** Be respectful of the parties and other judges. Do not engage in personal attacks or use disparaging language. Criticism is more effective when it is not cloaked in hyperbole.
5. ***Wordiness.*** Be concise, not verbose.

F. Sentence Structure

1. ***Adverbs.*** Place adverbs before verbs. (Bad: "He assumes erroneously that the list is exhaustive." Good: "He erroneously assumes that the list is exhaustive.")
2. ***Capitalization.*** Capitalize the titles of specific documents, but not the generic names of documents. You should capitalize "court" only when referring to the United States Supreme Court or the full name of a court.

3. ***Colons.*** Two spaces should follow a colon. The first letter following a colon should be lowercase unless the phrase following the colon is a complete sentence.

4. ***Commas.*** Generally, insert a comma before the conjunction "but" when it is used in a sentence. But a comma is not necessary in a short sentence. (Example: "The government's argument is sensible but ultimately unpersuasive.") Also insert a comma before "which" when it is used within a sentence as a relative pronoun.

5. ***Double negatives.*** Avoid sentences with double negatives. (Bad: "This does not mean that he is not disabled." Good: "This does not preclude a finding that he is disabled.")

6. ***Em dashes.*** You may use an em dash in a sentence to indicate a parenthetical thought. Place an em dash by inserting three hyphens.

7. ***First and last words.*** No two consecutive sentences should begin or end with the same word.

8. ***Hard spaces/hyphens.*** As a general rule, Judge G does not like hyphens, numbers, or symbols dangling at the end of a line. Specifically, you will need to place a hard space (by holding down the control button while you strike the space bar) between numbers in an *enumerated series* and the word immediately following the number. For example, if your sentence included a list of factors such as "(1) seriousness of the offense, (2) characteristics of the defendant," you would need to insert one hard space between "(1)" and "seriousness," and a second hard space between "(2)" and "characteristics." You also need to insert a hard space between a *record citation* and the cited page or document number. For instance, if you cite "DE 32 at 5," insert a hard space between "DE" and "32." Similarly, if you cite "JA 289," insert a hard space between "JA" and "289." Place a hard space between *symbols* (such as § or ¶) and their corresponding

numbers ("§ 1983"). In addition, insert hard spaces between the periods in an ellipsis to avoid breaking the *ellipsis* over two lines. In Word, a hard space can be created using ctrl + shift + spacebar (i.e., hitting the spacebar while holding the control and shift keys down). The shortcut in WordPerfect is ctrl + spacebar. Finally, place a hard hyphen between *number ranges* ("7-10"). In Word, the shortcut is ctrl + shift + -. The WordPerfect shortcut is ctrl + -.

9. *Headings.* Capitalize only the first word in a heading or subheading.

10. *Identifying the lower court.* When you first describe a lower court in a paragraph, identify the specific court ("bankruptcy court," "district court"). You should then use "the court" throughout the remainder of the paragraph, unless either you mention another court within the same paragraph or use of "the court" would otherwise be confusing.

11. *Introductory clausitis.* Do not begin more than two consecutive sentences with an introductory clause.

12. *Length.* Shorter sentences are better than longer sentences. Vary the length of sentences.

13. *Lists.* Use serial commas in a list of three or more items. (*Example*: "Despite his disability, Smith could walk, run, and swim.") Do not use semicolons, unless one or more of the individual list items contain commas (semicolons are okay in other contexts, of course).

14. *Passive voice.* Feel free to occasionally use the passive voice, especially if the meaning is clear and an awkward present-tense phrasing would otherwise result.

15. *Possessives.* Avoid using two or more possessives in a row (for example, do not use "Smith's mother's house").

16. *Sentence spacing.* Two spaces should follow the period at the end of each sentence.

17. Split infinitives. If splitting an infinitive sounds more natural, then split it.

18. Transitions. Do not begin sentences with "however" or "therefore." (Put these terms in the body of the sentence instead.) Sentences may, however, begin with "And," "But," and "Moreover."

19. Verb Tense. Be careful to use the correct verb tense. This problem comes up most often with the present tense: you should use the present tense where a fact is still true or where the described thing is still in existence.

G. Word Use

1. Preferred and Disfavored Words

Approximately. Use "approximately" instead of "about." (Example: "The package weighed approximately four grams.") "About" means "regarding" and should be used accordingly.

Attorney fees. Use the phrase "attorney fees," not "attorney's fees," "attorneys' fees," or "attorneys fees."

Because. Do not use "as" as a substitute for "because."

Court/judge. Describe the actions of the lower court ("the district court") rather than the judge ("the district judge"), unless context requires you to refer to the judge individually.

Even though. Use "even though" instead of "despite the fact that."

Finally. Use "finally" instead of "lastly."

In addition. Use "in addition" instead of "additionally."

Pleaded. Use "pleaded" rather than "pled."

Present case. As a general rule, use "in the present case" instead of "here." But use both phrases where one would otherwise appear numerous times in a confined space.

Record. Use "in the record" rather than "on the record."

Regarding. Use "regarding" or "concerning" instead of "as to."

Stated. Stated is a fairly nondescript word. If possible, use another word, such as "reasoned," "concluded," "explained," etc.

Words to avoid. Avoid the words "merely" and "some." Use "clearly" and "thus" sparingly.

2. **Word Usage**

    Abbreviations. Do not put quotation marks around abbreviations, i.e., (ERISA), not ("ERISA").

    Caselaw. Judge Gilman prefers to use "caselaw" as one word, not two.

    Compound adjectives. Hyphenate most compound adjectives ("independent-source doctrine," "ineffective-assistance-of-counsel claim," "narcotics-detection dog"). But do not hyphenate an adverb ending in -ly. ("properly pled complaint," "particularly described property"). And do not hyphenate compound adjectives that are used most commonly without hyphenation ("district court ruling," "due process clause," "good faith effort," or "summary judgment order").

    Court identifiers. Use "this court" when referring to prior decisions of the Sixth Circuit; use "we" when referring to the present case. Never use "we" in a bench memorandum. The "Supreme Court" means the U.S. Supreme Court. References to the supreme court of a state should include the name of that state (e.g., "the Michigan Supreme Court").

Criminal convictions. A defendant is convicted *on* a particular count ("Smith was convicted on count four of the indictment"), but is convicted *of* a specific crime ("Smith was convicted of conspiracy to possess and distribute cocaine").

Dates. Use "October 1998" and not "October, 1998" or even "October of 1998." Also, do not as a matter of course include a comma after a full date, unless the comma would otherwise be appropriate in the sentence. (*For example:* "Unlike the evening of August 30, 2005, the evening of August 31, 2005 was hot and rainy.")

Describing certain court actions. Courts make factual *findings* and reach legal *conclusions*. *Holdings* are dispositive rulings.

Distinctions. Observe the distinctions between the following terms:

that (defining/restrictive)	*which* (nondefining/nonrestrictive)
where (place)	*when* (temporal)
because (causal)	*since* (temporal)
although (contrast)	*while* (temporal)
may (permissive)	*might* (potential)

English words. Use English words whenever possible. (Bad: "Smith alleged, inter alia, that Jones had violated her constitutional rights." Good: "Smith alleged, among other things, that Jones had violated her constitutional rights.")

It. Do not use "it" as an indefinite pronoun. (Bad: "It goes without saying that Bob is a generous man.")

Last names. When referring to parties with the same last name — for instance, Elvis Presley and Priscilla Presley — you can use "the Presleys" to refer to the group, and "Elvis" and "Priscilla" to refer to the individuals.

Latin words and phrases. Common Latin words are not italicized, such as habeas corpus, de novo, sua sponte, etc. Never use the Latin words "supra" or "infra." Use "above" or "below" instead. Uncommon Latin words and phrases, such as *in abstentia,* should be italicized.

Names ending in "s." An individual whose last name ends in "s" takes the possessive form of apostrophe plus "s." But the plural possessive is indicated by only an apostrophe. (*Example*: "John Woods's dog is named Spot." On the other hand, "The Bonds' family dog is named Sandy.")

Numbers. Spell out numbers less than 10, unless there are higher numbers in the same sentence that the lower numbers are being compared to.

Only. Be sure that "only" is modifying the correct word. (Bad: "Relief is only available if both conditions are met." Good: "Relief is available only if both conditions are met." Bad: "The package only contained cocaine." Good: "The package contained only cocaine.")

Party names. Avoid formalistic names for the parties. (Use "Jones" instead of "Plaintiff-Appellant.")

Prefixes. Avoid hyphenating prefixes, unless a visual monstrosity results. ("Postconviction" is fine. "Prepresidential" is not.)

Series. Names or concepts in a series or list should appear in alphabetical order, unless another organizing principle would make more sense given the context.

Standard of review. When explaining the standard of review that the court applies, do not say that the court "reviews for clear error" or "reviews for abuse of discretion." Judge G instead prefers that you say that this court reviews the district court's judgment "under the clear-error standard" or the "abuse-of-discretion standard." In the case of de novo review, however, you may say that this court "reviews de novo a district court's grant of summary judgment."

That. Use the relative pronoun to avoid miscues. (Bad: "The government charged the lease deal sprang from a web of deceit." Good: "The government charged that the lease deal sprang from a web of deceit.") Do not, however, use more than two "that"s in a row in a sentence. Rephrase or eliminate one of the relative pronouns to avoid this result.

H. Citation Style

1. *Alterations to quoted text.* When removing alterations from a quotation, such as brackets or an ellipsis, indicate the specific alterations omitted in a parenthetical. Also indicate if you remove any citations or quotation marks within the same parenthetical, and list all of these items in alphabetical order.

    A special note regarding omitted quotation marks. When omitting quotation marks, include the word "internal." In other words, your parenthetical would be "(internal quotation marks omitted)." Also, be careful not to use "quotations" instead of "quotation marks."

    Some examples.

    (brackets and ellipsis omitted)

    (citation and internal quotation marks omitted)

(brackets, citations, ellipses, footnotes, and internal quotation marks omitted)

2. ***Citing and quoting parentheticals.*** You should use a "citing" parenthetical only if the additional source is particularly relevant (for example, the source is a Supreme Court case, a bedrock Sixth Circuit case, or a case from a specialized court). Use a quoting parenthetical, however, if you are quoting language that is itself quoting another source.

Note that, per Bluebook Rule 5.3(c), "citation omitted" is appropriate where the citation is being left out of the quoted portion of text. A different situation arises, however, where the quoted language quotes another source, but the citation to this underlying source is *not* itself part of the language that you are quoting. In this situation, Bluebook Rule 5.2(e) recommends using a quoting parenthetical rather than omitting quotation marks and using "internal quotation marks omitted" and "citation omitted" parentheticals. In the 20th edition, Bluebook Rule 1.5(b) no longer recognizes the use of the "internal quotation marks omitted" parenthetical. Bluebook Rule 5.2(f) allows for the omission of internal quotation marks only when the opening mark appears at the beginning of the language that you are quoting and the closing mark appears at the end of the language.

For example, suppose you want to quote the following language from *International Dairy Foods Association v. Boggs*, 622 F.3d 628, 635 (6th Cir. 2010): "By contrast, the decision of whether to grant a motion for a preliminary injunction is 'left to the sound discretion of the district court.' *Deja Vu of Cincinnati, L.L.C. v. Union Twp. Bd. of Trs.*, 411 F.3d 777, 782 (6th Cir. 2005)." According to 5.2(e), you would cite it as follows: "By contrast, the decision of whether to grant a motion for a preliminary injunction is 'left to the sound discretion of the district court.'" *Int'l Dairy Foods Assoc. v. Boggs*, 622 F.3d 628, 635 (6th Cir. 2010) (quoting *Deja Vu of*

Cincinnati, L.L.C. v. Union Twp. Bd. of Trs., 411 F.3d 777, 782 (6th Cir. 2005)).

3. ***Emphasis added (when citing to something in the record).*** When the emphasis-added descriptor does not directly follow a citation, such as in an opinion where you have deleted the record citation for the quotation, treat it as an abridged sentence and place it in parentheses, with the "e" capitalized. (*Example*: [big long block quote] (Emphasis added.)) Note that the period is placed inside of the parentheses.

4. ***Emphasis in original.*** In a rare break from the Blue Book, Judge G prefers that you indicate parenthetically if the emphasis in a quoted source is from the original text.

5. ***Hard spaces.*** Do not split section marks (§) and their section numbers across lines. To avoid this, insert a hard space. This rule also applies to not splitting JA citations from their page numbers, or docket entries from their entry number, or a list of numbers from their accompanying items. In Word, a hard space can be created using ctrl + shift + spacebar (i.e., hitting the spacebar while holding the control and shift keys down). The shortcut in Word Perfect is ctrl + spacebar.

6. ***Other opinions, references to.*** Cite as either "Maj. Op." (when dissenting or when concurring in part and dissenting in part), "Lead Op." (when concurring), or "Dissenting Op." (when writing the majority). *Example*: The majority also states that the Jehovah's Witnesses "may spread their message at stores, on street corners, in restaurants, in parks, and other public forums." (Maj. Op. at 21)

7. ***Parenthetical explanations.*** Include these as often as possible after a case citation unless they would be unnecessarily duplicative of the cited proposition or sentence. Remember not to omit articles such as "the," "a," and "an" from the parenthetical. Begin these parentheticals with a gerund, unless you are quoting a complete sentence.

8. ***Parts, references to.*** When referring to a portion of a memorandum or opinion, place periods after both the Roman numeral and the subpart letter or number. (*Example*: "As discussed above in Parts II.B. and III.A.2., this argument is without merit.") Use the word "Part" instead of the word "Section," and always capitalize "Part."

9. ***Pincites.*** Judge Gilman prefers that you not use pincites when summarizing the facts of an opinion unless you quote directly from the opinion. (*Example*: "The plaintiff in *Smith v. Jones* was a quadriplegic and blind in one eye." This does not require a citation to *Smith*. *But*: "She became a quadriplegic after a reckless driver 'sped through a stop light and collided with her vehicle'" would require a pincite to *Smith*.)

10. ***Record citations.*** Cite the record in parentheses. (*Example*: "When Burt provided a price acceptable to Holland, they shook hands and announced their agreement to the rest of the members at the meeting. (JA 934-35)") No periods should appear either inside or outside of the record citation. Remove citations to the record before submitting an opinion for filing.

11. ***Signals.*** When using the signal "*See, e.g.*," italicize everything except for the last comma.

12. ***Small caps.*** Do not use small caps. Use regular Roman type instead.

13. ***String cites.*** Use sparingly and, if used, include explanatory parentheticals.

14. ***Textual citations.*** When you refer to a case for the first time in a textual sentence, include the full case citation within that sentence.

15. ***Two-page rule.*** A source should be cited in full, even if previously cited in full, where that source has not been referred to in the prior two pages of text. The only exception is when

the case cited is well known and repeatedly cited, such as *Miranda* or *Terry*.

16. *Unpublished opinions.*

For opinions available via online databases only, follow this example: *Lyons v. TVA*, No. 87-5309, 1988 WL 12227, at *1 (6th Cir. Feb. 16, 1988).

For unpublished opinions available both in the Federal Appendix and online, cite to the Federal Appendix: *Lyons v. TVA*, 8 F. App'x 31 (6th Cir. 1998).

For opinions that have been designated for publication but have yet to be assigned to a federal reporter, follow this example: *Roberts v. Ward*, No. 05-6305, — F.3d —, 2006 WL 3392620, at * 2 (6th Cir. Nov. 27, 2006).

17. *U.S. Sentencing Guidelines.*

When used in text. The first time that you mention the federal sentencing guidelines, refer to them as the United States Sentencing Guidelines. After the first mention, you may thereafter refer to them as "the guidelines." You do not need to provide this shortened form in a parenthetical after the first reference.

When used in a citation. Follow Bluebook Rule 12.9.4 when citing to the guidelines, with the following considerations in mind. The text of a guideline is usually followed by commentary (abbreviated as "cmt.") The commentary includes all explanatory information that follows a guideline, and it often contains subsections for "Application Notes" and "Background" information. When citing to information that appears under the subheading of "Background," cite as U.S.S.G. § 2D1.2 cmt. background. Cite any numbered note in the commentary section—whether it appears under "Application Note" (*see, e.g.,* U.S.S.G. § 3D1.4) or not (*see, e.g.,* U.S.S.G. § 3D1.5)—as U.S.S.G. § [section number] cmt. n.1. And cite to a guidelines appendix as

U.S.S.G. app. C.

Exception: The Bluebook citation format refers to the guidelines as "U.S. Sentencing Guidelines Manual"—e.g.,.S. Sentencing Guidelines Manual § 3D1.1. When citing the guidelines in bench memos and opinions, you should instead use either "United States Sentencing Guidelines" (in the first reference to the guidelines, either in text or a citation) or "U.S.S.G." (if "United States Sentencing Guidelines" has already been referenced in either the text or an earlier citation).

Exception: Specify the guidelines version (i.e. 2010, 2015, etc.) only when relevant to the discussion.

Index

Institutional:

Amazon, pp. vi, vii, 1, 2, 4, 134, 135

Amazon CreateSpace, pp. vi, vii, 1, 4, 134

American Bar Association (ABA), pp. 55, 57, 70, 73

Board of Directors, pp. 4, 9, 10, 17, 23, 24, 25, 31, 33, 42, 54, 58, 59, 70, 116, 117, 131, 136

Chicago, pp. 6, 10, 18, 23, 24, 25, 30, 31, 52, 53, 54, 55, 56, 58, 59, 66, 67, 116, 118, 120, 123, 124, 131, 135, 136

Class actions, p. 128

Consultants, pp. 18, 23, 24, 25, 41, 42, 43, 52, 53, 54, 116, 117, 122

Courtroom5, pp. 27, 29, 61, 62, 64, 65, 78, 123

CT Corporation, pp. 13, 17, 18

Dispute Resolution Group; see also Stout Rissius Roth, pp. 53, 59

Downtown office suite—227 West Monroe, 50th floor, pp. 18, 20, 21, 23, 24, 25, 31, 32, 33, 54, 55, 114, 131

Feedback from members of Justice for Pro Se's, pp. 21, 38, 39

501(c)(3) nonprofit charitable foundation, pp. 9, 10, 12, 14, 15, 16, 20, 22, 23, 25, 37, 39, 40, 42, 60, 116

"Ghostwriting", pp. 38, 42, 61, 64, 70

Improving the Federal Judiciary, pp. 1, 2, 74, 116, 136

Intake information, pp. 32, 33, 34, 41, 71, 126, 127

Justice for Pro Se's, pp. vii, viii, 2, 3, 4, 7, 8, 11, 12, 13, 14, 15, 22, 23, 28, 30, 32, 33, 42, 52, 55, 56, 58, 66, 67, 115, 117, 119, 121, 129, 131, 132, 133, 137, 138

as 501(c)(3) nonprofit company, pp. 9, 10, 12, 14, 15, 16, 20, 22, 23, 25, 37, 39, 40, 42, 60, 116

Donations to Justice for Pro Se's, pp. 9, 10, 11, 12, 14, 15, 20, 21, 22, 25, 42, 60, 64, 83, 116, 117, 130, 131, 136

Impending change of name of company to Justice for Pro Se's pp. viii, 2, 3, 4, 7, 13, 72, 137

Office suite of, on 50th floor of 227 West Monroe St. in downtown Chicago, pp. 18, 20, 21, 23, 24, 25, 31, 32, 33, 54, 55, 114, 131

registration of by Illinois Attorney General, pp. 11, 13, 14, 17, 18

Staff (membership) of, pp. 4, 23, 24, 25, 26, 31, 37, 38, 40, 44, 82, 116, 128, 132

Legal ethics, pp. 32, 57, 61, 69, 70, 71
List 1, p. 76
List 2, p. 78
List 3, pp. 82, 83, 130, 131
Maps, pp. 36, 122
Office suite; see Downtown office suite, above
Polsinelli Law Firm, pp. 99, 121
Posner, Richard A., pp. 2, 3, 4, 7, 8, 9, 12, 16, 17, 18, 19, 20, 22, 26, 27, 32, 33, 34, 44, 56, 57, 58, 62, 72, 77, 115, 118, 126, 133, 134, 136
   compared to Oliver Wendell Holmes, p. 26, 27
   previous books by, relating to the subject of this book:
     Reforming the Federal Judiciary, pp. 1, 2, 74, 141
     Improving the Federal Judiciary, pp. 1, 2, 74, 116, 136
Prisons and police custody, pp. 32, 34, 60, 61, 66, 67, 74, 75, 116, 127, 129
Pro se, pp. 1, 2, 3, 4, 7, 9, 10, 23, 24, 26, 27, 28, 29, 30, 32, 33, 34, 37, 38, 39, 42, 43, 52, 60, 62, 63, 64, 74, 75, 83, 115, 116, 117, 123, 127, 128, 133, 134, 137
   Latin term meaning for oneself, pp. 1, 29
   Legal meaning: litigant who has no lawyer, p. 1, 60, 61
   The Pro Se Manual, pp. 43, 44, 45
Rationale for this book, pp. 2, 11, 24, 30, 37, 54, 129
Reforming the Federal Judiciary, pp. 1, 2, 74, 141
Regional Direction and Regional Directors, pp. 5, 6, 30, 39, 117, 118, 119, 120, 121, 122, 123, 131, 136
Roosevelt, Franklin Delano, p. 27
Screening applicants for assistance from Justice for Pro Se's, pp. 60, 61, 71, 127
Stout Rissius Roth LLC, pp. 53, 54, 57, 59, 60

U.S. Court of Appeals for the Seventh Circuit, pp. 1, 2, 3, 4, 7, 26, 27, 55, 58, 69, 70, 78, 115, 139
University of Chicago Law School, pp. 9, 11, 12, 18, 23, 24, 42, 52, 53, 56, 57, 67, 70, 116, 133, 135
Web Preview, pp. 138–148
Writing rules: see Judge Ronald Lee Gilman, below

Biographical:

Abeyta, Stephen, pp. 78, 125
Abraham, Ken, pp. 53, 61, 66, 67, 70, 71, 75, 78, 89, 125, 128
Acevedo, Philip, pp. 11, 12, 14, 16, 18, 19, 20, 22, 32, 52, 53, 133
Bazelon, Emily, p. 26
Bond, William C., p. 97
Broadhurst, Dan, pp. 53, 54, 57, 59
Bruer, Robert, pp. 66, 77, 82, 83, 88, 108
Carbide, Sakina, pp. 6, 61, 78, 93, 118, 120, 122
Clardy, Michelle, p. 121
Clark, Paul, pp. 6, 102, 122, 124
Collins, Patrick M., pp. 52, 53
Colpoys, Lisa, p. 54
Cook, James V., pp. 77, 91, 120, 125
Crush, Brian, pp. 11, 12, 16, 18, 19, 20, 21, 23, 32, 52, 53, 133
Dart, Thomas J., pp. 52, 53
DeBofsky, Mark, pp. 52, 53, 55, 58
DeMatteis, Claire, p. 53
Dowd III, George T., pp. 17, 55, 57, 77,
Dowd, Matthew, pp. 6, 16, 30, 78, 118, 124, 126
Durkin, Kevin P., pp. 52, 53
Ebron, Sonja, pp. 27, 28, 62, 63, 64, 65, 78, 123, 124
Ewing, Maura, p. 40
Fitzgerald, Patrick, p. 53
Foster, Michael, pp. 99, 121, 124
Fuller, Bradley, pp., 61, 77, 120, 124
Gevorkian, Makar, p. 23

Gilman, Judge Ronald Lee;
his Writing Rules, pp. 149–174
Gottschall, Judge Joan B., pp. 55, 59
Groninger, Kate, pp. 19, 20
Hazel, Steven, pp. 23, 111
Hogin, Jesse, pp. 23, 67, 85, 97, 113
Holmes, Oliver Wendell, pp. 26, 27
Hopkins, Bruce R., pp. 11, 12, 15, 19, 21, 22, 23, 124, 132, 133, 134
Hopkins, Harry, p. 27
Hopwood, Shon, pp. 9, 61, 78, 124
Invited consultants, pp. 18, 23, 24, 25, 41, 42, 43, 52, 53, 54, 116, 117, 122
Invited directors, pp. 123–126
Jacob, Devon M., pp. 77, 125
Keller, Ashley, pp. 17, 55, 57, 79
Klerman, Daniel, pp. 9, 37, 77, 79, 125
Kornstein, Daniel J., p. 26
Lessig, Lawrence, pp. 9, 37, 78, 79, 80, 125
Link, Father David T., p. 53
Macfarlane, Katherine, pp. 75, 103
Martin, Ted, pp. 3, 137
McAdams, John, p. 23
McCabe, Michael E., Jr., pp. 69, 72, 73, 90, 97, 111
McKinney, Pamela, pp. 15, 78, 123, 129
Meyer, Benjamin, p. 23
Miles, Thomas J., pp. 9, 55, 78

Nou, Jennifer, pp. 25, 42, 80, 116
Popkin, Alan, pp. 6, 30, 61, 77, 120, 121, 124
Rendleman, Dennis, pp. 55, 57, 61, 69, 70, 71, 77
Rosenfield, Andrew, pp. 10, 17, 20, 21, 23, 55, 56, 58, 76, 131
Rumsey, George W., pp. vi, 2, 77, 117, 123, 134
Seidel, Selvyn, pp. viii, 4, 10, 17, 22, 55, 58, 59, 78, 131
Sidak, Gregory, pp. 37, 77, 79, 80, 124
Siegler, Alison, pp. 9, 53, 54, 77
Slone, Debra, pp. 27, 62, 63, 64, 65
Stone, Rebecca, pp. 9, 37, 78, 81, 125
Taxy, Samuel, p. 23
Thesing, Patrick, pp. 6, 61, 78, 121, 124, 127
Van Oort, Aaron, pp. 76, 79, 121, 125
Vukadinovich, Brian, pp. 5, 6, 11, 24, 29, 30, 31, 38, 39, 42, 43, 44, 61, 63, 65, 66, 70, 71, 77, 94, 118, 123, 124, 126, 127, 131, 132
Williams, Judge Ann Claire, p. 55
York, Danielle, p. 23
Yuan, Theresa, pp. 12, 13, 18, 21, 22, 25, 31, 32, 40, 67, 78, 116, 123, 137
Zarfes, David, pp. 9, 11, 12, 17, 32, 53, 54, 133, 134
Zell, Jonathan, pp. 6, 30, 78, 117, 118, 123, 149

www.ingramcontent.com/pod-product-compliance
Lightning Source LLC
Chambersburg PA
CBHW052254220526
45471CB00001B/328